8 Mentoring Sessions You Can't Afford to Miss

David Cottrell 지음 | 정호섭 해설

Monday Morning Leadership(Bi-lingual Edition)

펴   냄   2008년 4월 1일 1판 1쇄 박음 • 2008년 4월 5일 1판 1쇄 펴냄
지 은 이   데이비드 코트렐
해   설   정호섭
펴 낸 이   김철종
펴 낸 곳   (주)한언
            등록번호 제1-128호 / 등록일자 1983. 9. 30
주   소   서울시 마포구 신수동 63-14 구 프라자 6층(우 121-854)
            TEL. 02-701-6616(대) / FAX. 02-701-4449
책임편집   윤혜영 hyyun@haneon.com
디 자 인   김하늘 hnkim@haneon.com
홈페이지   **www.haneon.com**
e-mail   haneon@haneon.com
            이 책의 무단전재 및 복제를 금합니다.
            잘못 만들어진 책은 구입하신 서점에서 바꾸어 드립니다.
I S B N   978-89-5596-474-5 03740

Mr. Native 원서 읽기

Monday morning Leadership

8 Mentoring Sessions You Can't Afford to Miss

Monday Morning Leadership(Bi-lingual Edition)

Read, enjoy, and apply

To.

From.

원서를 읽어야 하는 이유

영어 공부 잘하는 비결?

직장인들에게 영어 공부는 평생 떠안고 가야 할 숙제다. 중학교부터 대학교까지 10년 넘게 영어를 해왔지만 듣기와 말하기는 커녕 읽기조차 쉽지 않다. 도대체 왜 읽기조차 정복되지 않는 걸까? 사람들은 읽다가 이해가 안 되어 막히면 읽기를 포기해버린다. 하지만 당신 혼자 그러는 것이 아니니 너무 의기소침해할 필요는 없다. 읽기는 누구에게나 어려우니까.

그렇다면 어떻게 해야 할까? 개인마다 차이는 있겠지만 과연 얼마나 '영어를 즐기고 시간과 열정을 쏟았느냐'에 달려 있다. 여기에 구체적인 팁 몇 가지를 알려주겠다.

1. 자신의 수준에 맞는 글을 읽어라. 남들 읽는다고 해서 영자

신문이나 두껍고 어려운 책을 읽을 필요가 없다.

2. 읽는 중간에 사전을 찾기 위해 멈추지 마라. 그러면 문맥의 흐름을 놓치게 되고 이해의 정도도 떨어지게 된다.

3. 단어 순서대로 읽어라. 우리말로 바꿔서 해석을 하려고 하는 순간 영어는 어려워진다. 그냥 영어 어순 그대로 읽고 이해해라.

4. 본인에게 필요한 정보, 재미있어 할 만한 글을 찾아라. 그러면 스스로 자연스럽게 동기부여가 될 것이다.

인내를 가지고 오랫동안 꾸준한 열정을 보여줄 때 영어를 읽는 눈, 듣는 귀, 말하는 입은 선물처럼 주어진다.

직장인들을 위한 안성맞춤형 주제와 난이도!

많은 사람들이 원서를 읽겠다고 마음먹고 책을 펼쳐들었다가도 모르는 단어나 해석하기 어려운 문장을 만나면 중간에 읽기를 포기하곤 한다. 영어 공부를 위해 원서를 고를 때는 주제와 난이도를 꼼꼼히 따져봐야 한다. 어휘의 난이도가 과연 나의 수준에 맞는지, 주제가 너무 딱딱하거나 혹은 유치하지 않은지 말이다. 이런 전제조건이 충족되지 않으면 한 문장 한 문장 읽어나가기가 힘겨워지고 학습효과는 기대할 수 없다.

이 책은 직장인 독자들이 관심을 가져야 할 자기계발이나 처세와 관련된 내용이다. 회사 업무 효율을 높이고 행복하게 일할 수 있도록 도와주는 재미있고 실용적인 내용이 펼쳐질 것이다. 그리고 막히는 부분이 없이 단숨에 읽을 수 있도록 오른쪽 페이지에는 원문을, 왼쪽 페이지에는 단어 설명과 문장 해설을 배치하였다. 이야기의 흐름이 끊기지 않도록 배려한 것이다. 또 중간 중간에 미국에서도 바로 써먹을 수 있는 회화 표현을 실었다. 마지막에는 한글 요약문을 실어 본문의 내용을 확인할 수 있도록 했다.

실의에 빠진 관리자들에게 희망과 용기를 주는 책

이 책에서 제프는 스승 토니와 함께 그가 고민하고 있는 모든 경영상의 과제들을 해결하기 위해 8가지 핵심주제를 학습한다. 토니의 가르침은 일방적인 지침도, 감동은 있지만 실행 방법은 없는 연설도, 현장과는 동떨어진 뜬구름 잡는 얘기도 아니다. 멘토 토니는 제프의 고민을 낱낱이 듣고 매주 격려와 칭찬과 자극과 과제를 주며, 제프 스스로 관리자에서 리더로 성장할 수 있도록 돕는다. 토니라는 가상의 멘토는 '멘토 부재의 기업 현실'에서 우리에게 아주 중요한 변화의 씨앗을 제시한다.

한국어판으로 출간되어 많은 독자들의 사랑을 받았던 《먼데이 모닝 리더십》을 이제 원서 그대로 만나 볼 수 있다.

Read a story that can help your career!

"…an excellent reference book that provides sound leadership principles."

T. Michael Glenn, President and CEO

FedEx Services

"Another insightful and inspiring work by David Cottrell. He brings home vividly what true leaders do for themselves and for others."

Michael W. Grochowski

Regional Commissioner

Social Security Administration

"Never has mentoring been so needed; never has there been a book to fill the need like Monday Morning Leadership."

Charlie "Tremendous" Jones

Author of Life is Tremendous

"… a wonderful story sharing lessons of how to walk the leadership talk."

Eric Harvey, President and CEO

Walk the Talk Company

"Developing the eight principles in this book will immediately help you fulfill the responsibilities of your leadership position in the most effective way possible."
Jack Kinder, Jr. and Garry D. Kinder
Kinder Brothers International

"… as insightful as it is concise. Its 'to the point' style provides a clear roadmap for becoming a better manager."
Dan Amos, Chairman and CEO
AFLAC, Incorporated

"… a practical, informative, step-by-step series of lessons packed with leadership techniques which are essential to success!
Ed Foreman
Executive Development Systems, Inc.
Former U.S. Congressman
Texas and New Mexico

"… presented in an entertaining and easy to retain format. Great book."

Ray Biggs, President and CEO

Security Finance Corporation

"A terrific guide on how to be a mentor and how to follow the advice of wise counsel."

Mark C. Layton, President and CEO

PFSweb, Incorporated

"… a wonderful journey with a mentor. It will help you achieve the success and happiness you desire. It's great!"

Brian Tracy

Author of Maximum Achievement

8 Mentoring Sessions You Can't Afford to Miss

Contents

relatively 비교적 **fortune 500 company** 〈포춘〉지가 매년 발표하는 500대 우수기업 **barely** 거의 ~하지 못하는, 아주 가끔 **business is slow** 일이 잘 풀리지 않는, 더딘 **pressure** 부담감, 압력 **unbearable** 견딜 수 없는, 참기 힘든 **to be honest** 솔직히 **overwhelm** 압도하다, 질리게 하다 **outnumbered** 넘치는, 그 수가 많은 **what if** 만약 ~라면

· · ·

You look so down in the office. What's with you?
I was in a slump
사무실에서 기운 없어 보이던데. 무슨 일 있어?
난 슬럼프에 빠졌어.

slump는 사업이나 개인적인 일 등에서 의욕이 떨어진 상태를 말한다.

Prologue

Two Years Ago …

Things were not going well. For several years, I had been a relatively successful manager for a Fortune 500 company, but now I was in a slump. I was working harder than I ever had, but I was going nowhere. I barely saw my kids. My marriage was suffering. My health was not the best. I was struggling in every part of my life.

At work, my team was also feeling the effects of my slump. People were upset. Business was slow—real slow—and the pressure on us to improve performance was rapidly hitting the "unbearable" level. To be honest, I was ready to give up, because my doubts about my leadership abilities were overwhelming the confidence I once had.

My questions outnumbered my answers. What if I wasn't the right person for a leadership position anymore? What if I had been successful in the past because of the great

at a loss 어쩔 줄 모르는, 당황하는 **judging** (주로 남의 행동이나 모습을) 판단하려는 **semi-retired semi** 사무실에 출근하지 않고 업무를 관할하는 것 **executive** 주로 업무결정권을 갖는 간부, cf)CEO(Chief Executive Officer, 최고경영자) **iota** 아주 조금, 눈곱만큼의 것 **legendary** 전설적인, 유명한 **turn around specialist** 기업회생 전문가(turnaround는 주로 실패에서 벗어나 성공하는 것을 의미함) **bankruptcy** 파산 **profitability** 수익성 **integrity** 정직, 청렴

• • •

I was at the point where I needed to talk to someone. '나는 얘기할 사람이 필요한 시점에 와 있었다'

He was definitely light years ahead in experience. '그는 분명 경력에 있어서 한참 앞서 있었다'

Success had not changed Tony one iota. '성공으로 인해 그는 조금도 변하지 않았다'

…serving on a business council to develop a code of integrity for business executive. '경영자들의 청렴에 대한 규정을 연구하는 경영자 협의회의 일원으로 일하는'

code of… 법을 나타내는 말로 사용된다. cf)code of Hammurabi '함무라비 법전'

economy? What if I was just extremely lucky?

I was at a loss.

I was at the point where I needed to talk to someone—someone who would listen and offer suggestions without judging me.

One Saturday on the golf course, I saw a friend of my dad's named Tony Pearce. Tony was a successful, semi-retired business leader who spent his time writing books and coaching top executives. I'm still not sure of his age. He looked only a few years older than I, but he was definitely light years ahead in experience.

Success had not changed Tony one iota. His warm personality, athletic good looks and charismatic personality were already legendary around our community.

Before his retirement, Tony was a "turnaround specialist," someone who was able to rescue companies from bankruptcy and lead them to profitability. He had been honored twice by various national organizations as "Entrepreneur of the Year" and was currently serving on a business council to develop a code of integrity for business executives.

During the course of his career, Tony had made millions. He was highly respected in the community because he

above reproach 나무랄 데 없는, 훌륭한 **utmost** 가장, 지극한 **call upon** 요청하다, 방문하다 **serve as a sounding board** 조언자의 역할을 하다 **aspired to be** 꼭 닮고 싶은 **sought-after** 많은 사람이 필요로 하는 **long way from** ~와는 거리가 먼 **wondered if** ~인지 아닌지 모르겠다 **since** =therefore, Because **high demand** 열렬한 요청 **debating** 고심, 고민 **careen** (통제가 안 되어)기울어진 **out of control** 통제불능

• • •

I just heard that Bob got axed because he was caught stealing from the company.

No way!! His integrity and ethics were above reproach.

밥이 회사 자금을 빼돌려서 회사에서 퇴출 당했다던데?

그럴 리가! 그분은 닿을 수 없을 만큼 정직하고 도덕적인 분이었는데.

gave so much of his time and money to help others. His integrity and ethics were above reproach.

My grandfather would have called him "a real gentleman." My father had the utmost respect for Tony and had often called upon him to serve as a sounding board during his own business career.

Tony was the type of person I aspired to be—wise, respected, confident and a highly sought-after speaker and mentor. But right now I was a long way from becoming the person I wanted to be.

When I graduated from college, Tony wrote me a congratulatory note that—for some unknown reason—I never threw away:

Tony had not seen me at the golf course, and it had been a few years since we had talked. I wondered if he would even remember me if I called him. I also wondered if he would take the time to meet with me since he was in such high demand by executives of major corporations all over the country.

After debating whether or not to call him, I finally decided that I had nothing to lose. My life was careening out of control and something needed to change.

I made the call.

be honored to ~를 영광으로 여기다

• • •

Now the learning really begins. ‘이제 진정한 배움이 시작되는 거야’
a few years had gone by and a lot had changed. ‘몇 년의 세월이 지나고
많은 것이 변해 버렸지’

> TONY PEARCE
>
> *Dear Jeff,*
>
> *Congratulations on your graduation from college. You have completed a wonderful period of your life. Now the learning really begins. I know you will be successful in the field that you choose.*
> *If you ever want to talk about personal or business issues, I would be honored to allow you to learn from my experiences…you just have to ask.*
>
> *Best wishes,*
>
> *Tony Pearce*

A little nervous as I dialed Tony's number, I also was afraid that he wouldn't remember me and there I'd be…feeling like a fool. Even if he did remember me, a few years had gone by and a lot had changed since he had sent

nerve 신경 **settle down** 진정되다, 가라앉다 **passed away** 돌아가셨다(pass away는 die보다 더 정중한 표현이다) **ironic** 반어적인 **catching up** 그 동안의 소식을 나눔 **be willing to** 기꺼이 ~할 **encountering** 부딪힌, 마주친 **significant time** 의미 있는 시간(주로 Quality time으로 많이 사용) **commit** 약속하다, 책임지다 **be glad to** 즐거이 ~하다

· · ·

Even though Dennis just started with the company, he acts like a big shot and tries to tell me what to do.
What a coincidence! He did exactly same thing to me!!

데니스 있지, 이제 갓 회사 업무를 맡았으면 마치 대단한 영향력을 주는 사람처럼 이래라 저래라 한단 말이야.

이럴 수가! 나한테도 똑같이 했어.

me that note. Maybe his offer was no longer on the table.

When he answered the phone, it only took a few seconds for my nerves to settle down and my fear to disappear. As soon as I said "This is Jeff Walters," he immediately knew who I was. He asked how Mom was doing since Dad passed away, and then he said he was honored that I would call.

I found it ironic that he used the same word—honored—that he had used in my graduation letter years ago. "What a coincidence," I remember thinking after we had finished our conversation.

After some catching up, I reminded Tony of his note from several years ago. I told him I was having some challenges at work and that I would like his advice...if he was still willing to talk with me.

After explaining some of the problems I was encountering, he agreed to work with me only if I would commit to two things:

1. Tony said that he was not interested in helping me solve my problems. He was interested in helping me become a better person and leader and that would require spending some significant time together. If I would commit to meeting with him every Monday

elated 굉장히 기쁜 consented to ~을 승낙하다, 동의하다 one-on-one 일
대일로(=man-to-man) after all 결국, 역시 rationalize 합리화하다 bow
out 그만두다, 물러나다 turn out 판명되다, 드러나다 as far as ~까지는,
~하는 한

                              · · ·

a few years had gone by and a lot had changed. '몇 년의 세월이 지나고
많은 것이 변해 버렸지'
gracefully bow out of the session. '조용하게 (토니와의 8주) 과정을 그만둬
야지'
never again crossed my mind. '두 번 다시 생각나지 않았다'

morning for eight weeks, he would be glad to help.

2. Tony also asked me to commit to teach others the lessons and experiences that he would be sharing with me. He said none of my problems were unique and that others could learn from my experiences.

I was elated Tony consented to work with me, one-on-one, for eight weeks. I asked if we could meet on Fridays instead of Mondays, but he said his schedule would not allow that. So, I agreed to both of his requirements. "After all," I rationalized, "if the Monday Morning Meetings don't go well, I can somehow gracefully bow out of the rest of the sessions."

As it turned out, those eight meetings — my "Monday Mornings with Tony" — were the best meetings I have attended in my life. The thought of "gracefully bowing out of the sessions" never again crossed my mind.

As far as my second commitment — to teach others — that is my reason for writing this book.

I am honored you are investing your time in reading "Monday Morning Leadership" and ask you, in turn, to teach others the wisdom Tony shared with me.

Enjoy the journey, apply what you learn, and continue to grow as you share my Monday mornings with Tony.

gloomy 우울한 **frankly** 솔직히 **somewhat** 다소, 조금 **cynical about** ~에
대해 냉소적인, 부정적인 **at best** 기껏해야, 잘해봐야 **make me feel better**
위로가 되는, 기분이 나아지는 **numerous** 많은 **to no one's surprise** 대단한
것은 아닌 **highly-touted** 우수한, 고평가된 **deep down I knew** ~을 깊이 깨
닫고 있는

• • •

I guess~ 주로 자신에 주장을 이야기하거나 말에 확신이 없을 경우에 사용된
다. cf) I guess you' re right. '네 말이 맞는 것 같아'
I was at a crossroads in my career. '나는 내 회사생활의 기로에 서 있어'
something was going to have to change, one way or another. '어떤 방식
이든지 뭔가 변화는 있어야 했다'
Get with it! '한번 해보자고!(=Go for it!)'
I chided myself. '난 내 자신을 다그쳤다'

The First Monday_

Drivers and Passengers

It was a rainy, gloomy day when I left home for my first meeting with Tony.

Frankly, I was somewhat cynical about whether meeting with Tony would really change things at work. At best, time with Tony would probably make me feel better about how things were going. I guess I really doubted he could do much to change how I managed. After all, I had worked for years for one of the best companies in the world and had been to numerous management development sessions. To no one's surprise, the impact of these highly-touted training sessions never lasted more than a short time.

I had to keep reminding myself—if things were great, I would have never called Tony in the first place. The truth was this: I was at a crossroads in my career. Deep down I knew that something was going to have to change, one way or another. "Get with it," I chided myself. "Executives

step out 잠시 자리를 비우다(일반적으로 전화상에서 많이 사용됨) **Gentlemen's Quarterly** 1년에 4번 출간되는 잡지(계간지) **fatherly** 아버지 같이, 다정한 **quick tour** 잠시 돌아보는 것, 여기서는 집안구경을 의미 **incredible** 믿기 힘든, 대단한 **admit** 인정하다, 받아들이다(주로 의지와 반대로 받아들일 수밖에 없는 상황에서 사용) **intimidated** 기에 눌린, 기세가 죽은 **get down to** (본론)으로 들어가다 **set ground rules** 기본적인 원칙을 정하다 **make the best use of** ~의 활용을 최대화하다

· · ·

Come and see. '와서 만나다' 라는 뜻으로 일반적으로 Go and see는 Go See 로 and를 생략하지만 Come and see에서 and는 생략하지 않는 것이 일반적이다. cf)Go see a doctor '의사에게 가보세요'
I was a little intimidated. '약간은 주눅이 들었다'

· · ·

I'd like to speak to Mr. brown. Is he available?
He stepped out for lunch.
브라운 씨와 통화하고 싶은데 자리에 계신가요?
점심식사로 잠시 자릴 비우셨습니다.

all over the country ask for Tony's counsel. You should consider yourself fortunate he has time to talk with you."

We had agreed to meet at 8:30. Because of the rain, I drove into Tony's driveway at 8:40. Tony was waiting for me at the door, looking like he just stepped out of Gentlemen's Quarterly.

"Hello, Jeff. Welcome!" he said, extending his hand and pulling me toward him for a fatherly hug. "I am honored that you would take your time to come and see me."

Tony asked me to come in and gave me a quick tour. His home was incredible. It was large but had a warm feel to it. After the tour, he took me to his library where he said we would be meeting for the next eight weeks.

There must have been over a thousand books on his library shelves. I noticed several pictures of Tony standing with well-known business leaders I immediately recognized. Some of the pictures were taken in the library where I was sitting. I must admit I was a little intimidated.

After several minutes of catching up, he said it was time to get down to business.

"Your time is valuable, Jeff," he began. "I think we need to set some ground rules for us to follow if we're going to make the best use of our meetings; so I took the liberty of

handle 다루다, 받아들일 수 있다

· · ·

Simple enough. '아주 명료하네요'
Let's get going. '진행합시다'
Tell me what brings you here after all this time. '당신을 결국 여기까지
오게 만든 문제를 얘기해봐요' 영어에서는 직접적으로 용건을 묻는 것을 피하
기 위해 bring이라는 표현을 사용한다. cf)Why do you come to Korea?(=What brings you to Korea?) '당신은 왜 한국에 왔나요?'

· · ·

The score is 2:0. Let's get going, or we'll lose the game.
We'd better get going if we want to arrive on time.
점수가 2:0이야. 제대로 하자고, 그렇지 않으면 우리가 질 거야
제시간에 도착하고 싶으면 가는 게 좋겠는걸.

get going은 회화에서 위의 두 가지 형태로 사용된다.

drawing these up while I was thinking about our sessions. See what you think."

He pushed a handwritten note across the table to me that listed three simple rules:

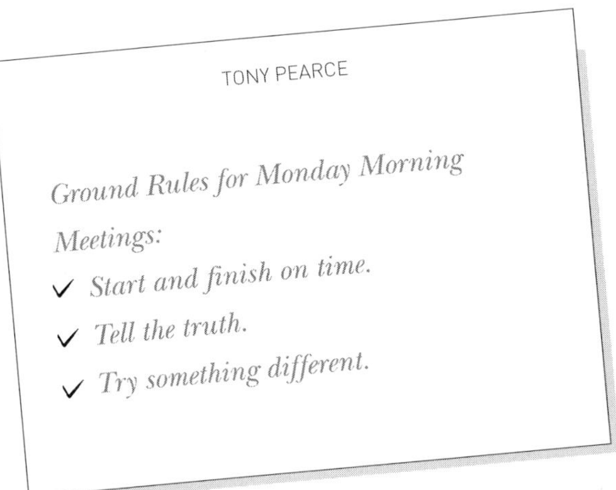

"Simple enough," I thought. "I can live with those rules." Then I looked back at Tony. "I can handle these. Let's get going."

"Okay then," Tony said. "Tell me what brings you here after all this time."

For the next hour, I did the talking and Tony listened without saying much.

energetic 활력이 넘치는 **optimism** 낙천, 낙관주의 **my first big break** 처음으로 찾아온 큰 기회 **early on** 초창기에 **acceptable** 수용할 만한, 인정받을 수 있는 **drive** 강한 본능이나 욕구, 열정 **performance issues** 업무수행상의 문제

· · ·

one of the guys 직역하면 '여러 사람들 중 한 명' 이라는 뜻이지만 여기서는 팀원들의 무리에 속하기 바라는 마음을 표현한 것이다.

· · ·

Give me a break! We just got here and you want us to leave already?
We've been working hard this morning. Let's take a break, OK?
좀 쉬게 해주세요! 이제 막 왔는데 가란 말씀이신가요?
오전 내내 열심히 일했으니, 잠깐 숨 좀 돌릴까요? 네?

I began at my college graduation, the last time we had spoken to each other. I had been so excited about the future; I felt there was nothing that would keep me from being successful. I was educated, energetic and full of optimism.

For the first few years of mycareer, success came easily and promotions were rapid. I worked in sales for one of the most respected technology manufacturing companies in the world.

Then I was promoted into management—my first big break—and I loved it. Business was good. I went on great trips. I was involved in making some big decisions, and I learned a lot, early on. My team was not top performing, but our results were acceptable, even more than acceptable.

Some of the people on my team didn't have the drive that I had, but business was so good that I didn't worry about them. Actually, I probably ignored some performance issues that contributed to the problems I had now.

Oh, and I tried really hard to be "one of the guys." I wanted my team to like me so they would want to work for me. So I frequently took them out for dinner and drinks— even shared some of the issues I was facing. At the time, it

upper managemen 상급 임원, 관리자 **go under** 일과 관련한 심각한 문제의 발생이나 실패 **intact** 그대로인, 변하지 않은 **look (someone) up** 방문하다, 찾아가다 **dejectedly** 낙심하여, 맥없이

· · ·

I'm at my wits' end. '나는 어찌할 바를 모르겠다'
our results reflected our frustrations. '우리의 좌절감은 성과에 그대로 반영됐다'

seemed like a good strategy.

About that same time, I believed the job upper management was doing was far from acceptable. In fact, I even told my team that if we did our jobs like upper management did theirs, our company would go under. We all laughed about that.

Those were the good times. But over the next several years, business began getting tougher. Most of my team was still intact, but some of the performance issues I once ignored were now affecting my division's performance in a big way —and by "big," I mean they were becoming threats to my job.

I was working hard—long hours—but the business indicators were telling me things were pretty bad. I wasn't very happy and the people on my team weren't happy. Our results reflected our frustrations.

"I looked you up, Tony, so I could learn from you," I said dejectedly. "I'm at my wits' end, and I hope it's not too late for me to turn this ship around."

He had listened for almost an hour when Tony finally started talking.

"First," he said, "I know you think these problems and the situation you described only exist on your team. You

perspective 견해, 관점 **riveting** 잡아끄는, 매혹적인 **insight** 통찰력, 식견

• • •

When it comes to leading people. ʻ사람들을 이끄는 입장에 서면ʼ
Donʼt (stop) feel sorry for yourself. ʻ자책은 이제 그만하게ʼ

• • •

Iʼm poor at negotiating(x)
Iʼm not good at negotiating(o)

비지니스 상에서 본인을 표현할 때 부정적인 단어사용을 피하고 긍정적인 단어를 부정하는 것이 좋다.

could not be more wrong. There are few—very few, if any—leaders who have not been faced with the same issues you've just shared. I know I have."

"When it comes to leading people, there is no problem that is unique to you. You could ask anyone with experience, and you would discover they have had to face the same issues, the same frustrations. So don't feel sorry for yourself. That's a waste of valuable time. Just make plans to make things better.

"Second, it's not too late to change," Tony continued. "You're still a young person even though you have a wealth of experience. I admire you for calling me and seeking advice. Few people have the courage to take that step."

"Obviously, you're facing some real challenges. Seeking an outsider's advice is a good move. We all need people who will help us look at situations from a different perspective," Tony said, his tone riveting my attention to every word. "In fact I have several people who are my mentors—people who have helped me gain new insights—and who have remained my mentors after all these years. It's not too late to change, but you will have to work to make improvements."

transition (~으로 이행하는) 변화 **extraordinary** 특별한, 비상한 **consistent** 일관적인, 꾸준한 **empathetic** 감정을 이해하는 **wanting to be liked**⋯ (남들이 자기를) 좋아하길 바라는 것

• • •

You're setting yourself up for failure somewhat along the way. '너는 스스로 어느 정도 실패의 여지를 만든 셈이다' set up은 주로 '차리다, 정하다' 의 표현이지만 많은 경우에 '자리를 마련하다, ~하도록 만들다' 의 뜻으로 사용된다. cf)Would you set me up with Daniel? '다니엘 씨 좀 소개해주시겠습니까?'

"Remember: You're not alone here. Most people have difficulty making the transition from employee to manager and from manager to leader. Your dad once told me something that I will never forget. He said that if you want to be extraordinary, the first thing you have to do is stop being ordinary. Wanting to be liked and 'just one of the guys' is natural. Of course, everyone likes to be liked. But as a leader, your team should like, or respect, you for the right reasons."

"If they like you because you're fair, consistent, empathetic, or a positive person—that's great. But if they like you just because you provide them with free dinners and drinks, what have you gained? You're setting yourself up for failure somewhere along the way. If your goal is to get everyone to like you, you will avoid making tough decisions because of your fear of upsetting your 'friends.' "

"Transitioning from employee to manager or manager to leader requires that you make different decisions. And believe me, those transitions can sometimes create challenges in every other area of your life as well."

"I remember when you were a teenager, Jeff. You were so excited when you celebrated your 16th birthday and got your driver's license. Remember? You had watched your

nod (one's head) 고개를 끄덕이다 **distraction** 산만함 **mess around** 빈둥대
다 **no longer** 더 이상 ~이 아닌

• • •

Would you stop messing around with your cell phone and get to work!
Excuse me? I'm sending a text message to our client now!
휴대폰 갖고 그만 빈둥대고 일 좀 하시지?
네? 전 지금 고객한테 문자 메시지를 보내고 있는 거라고요!

mom and dad drive for years, and as soon as you were old enough, you went through the driver's education course."

"Now, remember how confident you were? You knew that you would be the best driver ever. You even promised your dad with those very words," Tony said with a wink.

"Of course I do," I replied. "I also remember the second day after getting my license, I had an accident. Thankfully no one was hurt."

"I remember that, too," Tony nodded. "Most of your soccer team was in the car with you. But, what you don't know is that a few days later, your dad and I discussed that the main reason for the accident was your failure to understand the difference in responsibilities between being the driver and being a passenger."

"You see, passengers are free to do a lot of things the driver can't do. As a driver, your focus needs to be on the road and not on the distractions. As a driver, you no longer have the right to 'mess around' — like listening to loud music — even though it seems okay to do that as a passenger."

"The same principle applies when you become a leader. You're no longer a passenger; you become the driver. Even though your responsibilities increase when you become a

for instance 예를 들면, 가령 **pity party** 한심한 파티 **hard to swallow** 감당하기(받아들이기) 힘든 **speaking of** ~에 관해서 말한다면 **stumble** (말을) 더듬거리다 **make adjustment** 조절하다, 조치를 취하다

· · ·

He wasn't through. '그는 거기서 끝내지 않았다'
I said innocently. '나는 별 생각 없이 대답했다'

manager, you lose some of the rights or freedoms you may have enjoyed in the past."

"For instance," Tony continued, "if you want to be successful as a leader, you don't have the right to join employee 'pity parties' and talk about upper management. You lose the right to blame others for a problem in your department when you are a manager and leader. You are the person responsible for everything that happens in your department, and that can be pretty hard to swallow."

But he wasn't through. "You even lose the right to some of your time because you're responsible for other people's time as well as your own," he said, stopping to check his watch. "Speaking of time, what time did you arrive today?"

"A little after 8:30," I said innocently.

"And what time did we agree to begin?" Tony wondered aloud.

"Eight-thirty. But it was raining, and traffic was heavy, and I thought I left in plenty of time," I stumbled.

"Yes, it was raining," he easily agreed. "But the rain didn't make you late. You see, Jeff, when you accept total responsibility for whatever happens, you make adjustments. When it's raining, you leave earlier, or take a

force someone to ~가 ~할 수밖에 없도록 하다 **no matter what** 비록 ~일지라도 **control over** ~을 제어(관리)하다 **react to** ~에 반응하다   **eliminate** 제거하다, 없애다 **glance at** 곁눈질하다 **spiral note** 스프링 노트

• • •

You won't be able to put plans in place to accomplish your goals. ‘당신은 목표 달성을 위한 계획을 세울 수 없을 거예요’
Don't even have the word in your vocabulary. ‘그 단어(blame)는 당신의 사전에 담아두지도 마라’ 라는 뜻으로 ‘blame이라는 단어를 생각조차 하지 말라’ 는 의미로 해석할 수 있다.

different route, or call and change the meeting time. You control if you are on time or not. The rain just forces you to make different decisions."

"The opposite of accepting responsibility is to find someone or something to blame for the issues you're facing. Of course, there is always someone or something to blame, but a real leader spends his time fixing the problem instead of finding who to blame."

"What happens when you place blame is that you focus on the past. When you accept responsibility, you focus on this time forward—on the future. And Jeff, until you accept total responsibility—no matter what—you won't be able to put plans in place to accomplish your goals."

"One of the first things I want you to understand is that you have control over how you react to situations. If you eliminate blame—don't even have the word in your vocabulary—then you can make some positive changes."

Tony glanced at his watch again. "Well, I see we're about out of time today…as we agreed."

He handed me a blue spiral notebook with the words "Monday Mornings with Tony" handwritten across the cover. "Take this notebook and begin writing down what we discuss," he said. "It will be easier for you to keep

external factors 외부적인 요소(요인) **belly up to** 아주 가까이에 이르다
sheepishly 소심하게 **see how it goes** 상황을 지켜보다 **frustrated** 좌절한,
난감한

. . .

I'm not so sure I can 'belly up to the total responsibility bar'. '나는 내
가 완전한 책임의 관문에 다다를 수 있을지 확신이 서지 않아'

. . .

When could you call me for shipping schedule?
I'll call you 7:05a.m. sharp.
선적 스케줄에 대해서 언제 전화해주실 수 있나요?
정확히 오전 7시5분에 전화 드리겠습니다.

sharp가 시간과 같이 쓰일 때는 정확이 그 시간을 맞추는 것을 의미한다.

track of when you need to review our discussions."

Tony stood and walked me to the door. "So is there anything you will do this week to make your situation better?"

"Well, what you said about taking responsibility makes sense, but there are so many external factors working on my team, I'm not so sure I can 'belly up to the total responsibility bar,' " I said sheepishly.

"But what I can do, for sure, is not participate in the pity parties or blame upper management for our problems. And I will try to take responsibility for everything and see how it goes," I promised.

"Write those things in the notebook when you get home," Tony suggested. "And remember, when you write things down, you commit to doing them. If you simply tell me what you want to do, there is really no commitment to getting it done."

I agreed and told him I would be there at 8:30 sharp next Monday.

I left Tony, feeling even more frustrated. It was going to be pretty hard to accept responsibility for everything that happened in my department, and I wasn't sure it was realistic. Some of the things he had said made sense, but

up to date 최신의, 최첨단의 **courage** 용기 **tremendous** (양이나 크기가) 많
은 **blue print** 청사진, 계획

were his philosophies up to date, I wondered. But, I had promised. I would try something different and then wait to see what would happen.

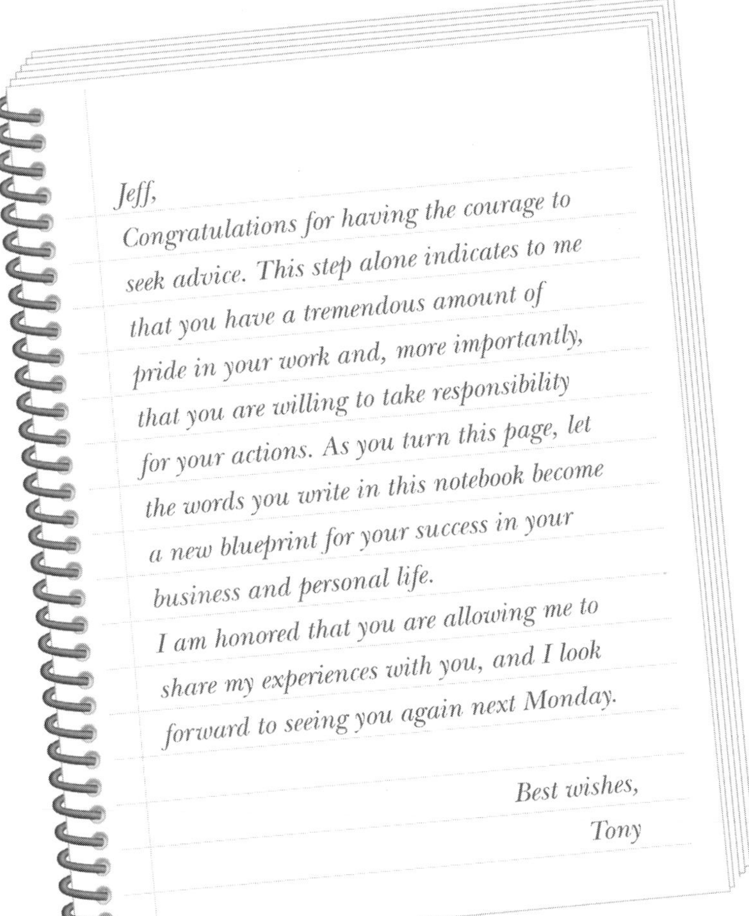

genuineness 진심 **sincerely** 진정으로

• • •

I began to feel more confident than I had in years that change for the good was on the horizon. '좋은 변화가 임박해오자 나는 몇 년 만에 더 많은 자신감을 느끼기 시작했다' on the horizon은 '지평선에' 라는 뜻이지만 여기서는 비유적 표현으로 '임박한, 분명해지고 있는' 의 의미로 쓰인다.

• • •

Steve always has valuable suggestions.
Yea, I agree and also I could feel the genuineness of his words.
스티브는 항상 기막힌 제안을 한단 말이야.
그래. 자네 말이 맞네. 그의 말에는 진정성이 있다는 것을 느낄 수 있어.

Later that day, I opened the notebook to record the lessons I had learned. Inside the notebook was a letter from Tony that read: As I read the note, I could feel the genuineness of his words. He sincerely wanted me to be successful. And I began to feel more confident than I had in years that change for the good was on the horizon.

**Transitioning from manager to leader requires that you make
different decisions.** '관리자에서 리더로 변화하는 데는 다른 종류의 결단이
필요하다'

BE A DRIVER:

✓ *Until you accept total responsibility—no matter what—you will not be able to put plans in place to accomplish your goals.*

✓ *Transitioning from manager to leader requires that you make different decisions.*

pouring down rain 쏟아 붓는 비, 폭우 **dash** 돌진하다 **ahead of** (시간적으로) ~보다 이전에 **swift trot** 빠른 걸음 **foyer** (서재 등의) 방

• • •

He smiled as he opened the door just ahead of my swift trot into his foyer. '그는 웃으며 나의 빠른 걸음보다 앞서 그의 서재 문을 열어주었다' **but the rats won the race again this week.** '이번 주에도 쥐가 경쟁에서 이기고 말았죠' 여기서 rat은 제프가 본인을 지칭한 것으로 자신이 완전한 책임을 지려고 했으나 쉽지 않았다는 의미이다.

Keep the Main Thing
the Main Thing

I drove into Tony's driveway at 8:20. It was pouring down rain again, and I waited for a couple of minutes before I dashed toward Tony's house.

He smiled as he opened the door just ahead of my swift trot into his foyer.

"Welcome," he said. "And good job! You made it with time to spare, and the weather is much worse than last week. Thanks for coming to my home, Jeff!"

"And it looks like you learned something about responsibility last week since you made some different decisions that allowed you to be here on time today," he added with a smile.

"Yes," I agreed. "I learned to leave home earlier, but I'm not sure I did very well with my people, Tony. I tried to accept total responsibility for everything happening in my department, but the rats won the race again this week.

get something done ~일을 마치다, 완성하다 **settle into** ~에 자리 잡다 **winged-back chair** 등받이 의자 **put it mildly** 조심스레 말하다 **spread out** (일을) 분산하다, 범위를 넓히다 **agitate** 휘젓다, 동요하다 **restless** 침착하지 못한, 불안한

• • •

Karen, my boss, is demanding—and that's putting it mildly! '내 상사 카렌은 좋게 말해서 요구가 지나친 사람입니다' demanding은 요구가 많은 사람의 성격을 의미하기도 한다.

but as soon as we put out one fire, another one pops up. 직역하면 '그러나 하나의 불을 끄자마자 다른 불이 치솟는다' 라고 해석할 수 있지만 이 문맥상으로는 '그만둔 사람의 공백을 채우자마자 다른 사람이 그만둔다' 로 이해할 수 있다.

Honestly, I have so many things coming at me from so many different directions, it's hard for me to get anything done…I mean done well."

"Tell me more," he said, settling into a comfortable winged-back chair.

"Well, I have fifteen people reporting to me," I began. "I also have two open positions. Karen, my boss, is demanding—and that's putting it mildly! I'm confident all my people know what they're supposed to be doing, but we seem to get less and less accomplished. We've spread out the responsibilities of the open positions to everyone on the team, but as soon as we put out one fire, another one pops up."

As I continued to speak, Tony seemed to become agitated and restless. "Are you okay?" I asked.

"Well, Jeff, it appears to me that everything is a crisis to you," he said. "Your job is not crisis management, and your people should not be firefighters. That said, I think there are some basic questions that require answers at this point:

- ✔ Why do you have two open positions?
- ✔ Why did these team members leave?
- ✔ Why do you think everyone on your team knows

priority 우선순위 **focus on** ~에 집중하다 **equip** 장비를 갖추다 **outst-**
anding 우수한 **pause** 잠시 멈추다 **sink in** 스며들다, 분석하다

· · ·

You'd better call HR and find out what happened.
I know and I want this to be very clear.
무슨 일인지 HR에 전화해서 확인해보게.
저도 압니다. 이번 일은 확실히 하고 넘어가야겠어요.

what they're supposed to be doing if they're not doing it?

✓ What are your priorities?

"Wait. Don't answer those questions now," Tony said. "Just think about them before next week.

"Now, let me tell you about one of my experiences," he continued. "I once worked with a manager who would remind us daily to 'keep the main thing the main thing.' The 'main thing' was our purpose or priority. Then he would ask us, 'So, what is the main thing?' And because every person on our team knew the main thing, this helped us focus on what was important.

"Actually, the main thing was really three things:

✓ Equip our employees with the tools to be successful.

✓ Provide outstanding service to our customers.

✓ Make a profit.

"If someone asked us to do something that was not part of our main thing, our manager would support us when we said that we couldn't get it done. We were a focused and productive workgroup because there was a clear understanding of our purpose."

Then he paused to let that sink in before he continued our meeting. "You mentioned that your people know what

perception 견해, 인지 **salary administration** 급여체계 **resignation** 사직
meet one's needs ~의 요구에 부합하다 **in most instances** 대부분의 경우에
speaking of ~을 말하자면 **necessarily** (필연적인 결과로) 반드시

• • •

It's a natural tendency. '그건 자연스런 경향이야'
I'm not saying that's the case here. '당신의 경우가 그렇다고 말하는 것은
아니에요' I'm saying that은 자신의 말에 대한 확신을 갖고 상대방이 받아들
일 것을 요구할 때 사용한다.

to do. Why don't you ask them, 'What is the main thing?' They probably have different perceptions of what the main thing is.

"I have found that when you depend on another's perceptions to match your expectations, you're setting yourself up for disappointment. Ask some questions…you may be surprised by your team members' answers."

"We'll spend another Monday on the importance of hiring the right people for your team; but now, I think you should try to understand why people chose to leave your team. It's a natural tendency (but not an accurate perception) to blame pay, benefits, upper management, salary administration, and other factors for someone's resignation."

"Now listen carefully because I want this to be very clear: People normally don't leave because of those reasons. People leave because their manager is not meeting their needs. People quit people before they quit companies. I'm not saying that's the case here; however, I am saying that in most instances the boss is the principle reason people resign."

"Speaking of bosses, you said Karen is a demanding boss. That's not a bad thing necessarily. I've heard many

get in the way 방해하다, 가로막다   **provide recognition** 포상하다   **reg-ardless** ~을 고려하지 않더라도

• • •

That's just it. '그것이 전부다' that's it이라는 표현을 강조하기 위해 just를 붙이기도 한다.
These are not option. '이것들은 선택사항이 아니다'

bosses called much worse. So how would you describe your relationship with Karen?"

"Well, that's just it. We really don't have much of a relationship. We have monthly meetings and that's about it. Karen is demanding because she's extremely results focused and is always requesting reports and information. I think she tends to get in our way."

"What are your expectations of Karen?" Tony asked.

"I think she should be a better leader. She should take the time to meet with me, provide recognition for my team, communicate with me, and help me be better at my job. After all, she's supposed to be my mentor. She doesn't do any of that—she's only interested in reports and results."

"Jeff, you're probably right. Maybe she should do a better job in those areas. Regardless, you still have fifteen people who are depending on you to develop a positive relationship with Karen. Your job is to inform her about what is going on in your department and achieve results. These are not options. For you to be successful and provide your employees with the necessary tools for them to be successful, you and your boss must work together— no matter what."

"I can understand why you think it's Karen's responsi-

subordinate 부하직원 **volunteer** 자진해서 (솔직히) 말하다, 시인하다

· · ·

It's up to you to make some change to make it happen. '일의 실현을 위해 변화를 꾀하는 것은 당신이 해야 할 일이다'

bility to develop a positive relationship with you—and you're right. However, if it's not happening, it's up to you to make some changes to make it happen.

"I suggest that you take the time to manage your boss the same way you manage your subordinates. Find out specifically what she needs from you and tell her specifically what you need from her. Do you know what her main things are? Does she know what your main things are? It may be worth a meeting to understand what both of you can do to help each other accomplish your main things."

"Okay, Jeff. Our time is about over for this week's meeting; so what are you going to do differently before next Monday?" Tony asked.

"Clearly, I think you're right about my team not knowing what the main thing is," I volunteered. "In fact, I'm not sure I know what the main thing is myself. So, my first job is to figure out what the main thing is and have a meeting to discuss it with the team."

"I will also try to meet with Karen to find out what I can do to help her accomplish her main thing. I will work on developing a positive relationship with her as best I can."

"I know we need more focus," I added. "I've let the cir-

dictate 지시하다

· · ·

I've let the circumstances dictate our actions rather than our mission dictating our actions. '나는 미션에 따라 행동하기보다는 환경에 따라 행동 해왔다'
Why do you have all these fire drills? 그만둔 직원의 공백을 채우는 일을 불 끄는 일에 비유했듯이, 여기서도 그만둔 직원의 공백에 대비해야 하는 상황 들을 화재훈련에 비유하고 있다.

cumstances dictate our actions rather than our mission dictating our actions."

"I'm also going to try to answer your questions. I have to admit I really don't think that I have two open positions because of me, but I will open my mind to that possibility," I concluded as we walked from the room.

As I left Tony's house, I couldn't get his words out of my mind: "What is the main thing? Why did two people resign? Why do you have all these fire drills?"

I had some work to do before the next Monday Meeting.

People quit people before they quit companies. '사람들은 회사를 떠나기 전에 사람을 먼저 떠난다'

WHAT IS THE MAIN THING?

✓ *People have different perceptions of what the main thing is.*

✓ *People quit people before they quit companies.*

dapper 말쑥한, 활기찬 **exit interview** 퇴직자 면접 **reveal** 드러내다

· · ·

I tackled the resignation issue head-on. '우선 나는 사임 문제에 정면으로 부딪혔다'

· · ·

This diet book we've been publishing is a cash cow.
Yea. I think things are getting better.
이 다이어트 책은 대박이야.
그러게요. 일이 잘 풀리고 있는 것 같아요.

Escape from Management Land

 "Good morning, Jeff."

Tony met me at the door for our third Monday Morning Meeting, looking as fresh and as dapper as ever. "You're on time and appear to be in a much better mood this week. I hope things are getting a little better at work."

"Well, I spent a lot of time on the three questions that I left here with last week," I said. "Much of my frustration has been not knowing what the problem was—much less what to do to fix it. I think I've made some real progress this week."

"First, I tackled the resignation issue head-on. I reviewed Jeni's and Chad's exit interviews. They both resigned during the past couple of months. And, just as I expected, the exit interviews didn't reveal much information. In fact, if you read each of the exit interviews without knowing what they were, you'd think both employees were happy to be

step further 한 단계 더 **reluctant** 마음 내키지 않는 **say up front** 정직하게 (솔직하게) 말하다

• • •

I knew you wouldn't buy that answer. 직역하면 '그 대답을 산다' 가 되겠지만, 그 말을 살 정도로 믿거나 이해하지 못하다는 것을 비유한 표현이다.

working here."

"Taking my search a step further, I talked to a few people on my team. And while they were reluctant to speak for their former teammates at first, one person—Michael—provided some interesting information," I reported.

"Michael said neither Jeni nor Chad really wanted to leave, but they were unhappy about things that had been going on in the company. Michael also reminded me both Jeni and Chad received increases in pay shortly before their resignations, so pay had little to do with their decisions to leave."

"Your words from last week kept ringing in my ears: 'People normally quit because their manager is not meeting their needs. People quit people before they quit companies.' Well, I still felt some circumstance was the reason they left—not me or something I did," I admitted. "But I knew you wouldn't buy that answer, so I went to see both Chad and Jeni."

"I met with each of them individually, and since they no longer work for me, there was no reason for them not to tell the truth. I'll say up front, both seemed surprised I was interested enough to go see them, and they opened up—more than I expected.

come right out (시간상) 곧바로, 즉시 **come down to** ~로 귀결되다 **lazy in** ~에 나태한, 적극적이지 않은 **abuse** 혹사시키다

· · ·

fog a mirror 직역하면 '거울을 뿌옇게 하다, 분명히 볼 수 없게 하다' 이지만 여기서는 '자신에 본모습을 감추다' 정도로 해석할 수 있다.

"I was shocked by what I heard. Well, they didn't come right out and say it, but I left knowing that they didn't leave the company; they left me—their manager. Just as you said, I wasn't meeting their needs. So during my visit with each of them, I took a lot of time trying to understand what needs I hadn't meet. Basically it came down to three things:

"First, hire good employees. Their perception was I had gotten lazy in my hiring. In fact, one of them said that if a person could 'fog a mirror,' I would select them for our team."

"The problem was my good employees were being asked to do more and more, while others were being asked to do less and less. Chad even said, 'Some of us felt abused because we were good employees.' Honestly, Tony, I couldn't believe what they were saying. Could I really be punishing the good employees by giving them more work and rewarding the lower performing employees by allowing them to do less? Both Chad and Jeni thought so…and thought so enough to leave.

"Second, coach every member of the team to become better. I walked away from both meetings upset with myself. I hadn't provided adequate feedback and direction

assume (사실이라고) 생각하다 **let down** 실망시키다 **dehire** 해고하다 **hu-
mble** 초라한, 열등감을 느끼는 **combine** 조합하다 **address into one** 하나로
정리하자면

. . .

Dehire the people who aren't carrying their share of the load. '자신의
역할을 하지 못하는 사람들을 해고하다' 자기 몫의 짐을 들지 못한다는 것은
제 역할을 하지 못하는 것을 의미한다.

to either of these employees, employees I considered among my best. Really, I assumed—I know what they say about assuming anything—they were happy working without much feedback. I think I let them down by not paying enough attention to their individual needs.

"And third, dehire the people who aren' t carrying their share of the load. I told you before about performance issues I had ignored. Well, those performance issues had an effect on the rest of the team. Jeni said what began as one negative and cynical employee became a whole team of negative and cynical employees. She said they kept looking to me to fix the problem, but I allowed it to go on...I did nothing."

"Needless to say, Tony, I was humbled after my meetings with Chad and Jeni. I was also a little relieved. At least I now know there are things I can do to avoid losing more good employees."

"I combined the other two questions you asked me to address into one: What is the main thing—the main purpose for our team?"

"Wednesday, I had a meeting with my team. I prepared a paper for each team member to complete. On the paper was one sentence: 'The main thing in our department

consistency 일관성 mass confusion 큰 혼란(혼동) take the initiative (남보
다)앞서서 ~하다 ego-builder 자긍심(자존심)을 중시여기는 사람 confess 인
정하다, 고백하다 exclaim 감탄하며 외치다

is…' and each person was asked to fill in the blank."

"Well, I know you won't be surprised by their answers, and really, neither was I. No one knew what the main thing was. Oh, everyone had an answer, but there was no consistency. This exercise showed me that instead of clearly defined goals and expectations, we had mass confusion about our most important mission as a team."

"So now I know our team has some work to do to define and understand the main thing. But, it seemed as though everyone felt good about having some direction established."

"I also had a good meeting with Karen. I think she appreciated me taking the initiative to meet with her. We still have a way to go, but I'm making it a priority to manage that relationship better."

"And yeah — I am in a better mood this week. I've realized there are things that I control that have contributed to my frustrations and the team's frustrations. Even though last week was not an ego-builder because of some of the answers I received, I do feel better. Now I know there is something that can be done, and it's something I can do," I confessed.

"Wonderful!" Tony exclaimed, although without surp-

stride 진전   **paralyze** 마비시키다   **contribute to** ~에 기여하다   **trap** 함정
fall into 빠져들다   **perspective** 견해, 관점   **comical** 우스꽝스러운

• • •

Did you see the way Kim and her team kiss up to the boss? Her team members told me they don't even like him, but they are hoping he'll give them a promotions.
Well, but things are not always as they seem.
김과 그 팀원들이 사장에게 아부 떠는 것 봤어요? 그 사람들이 그러는데 사실 사장을 좋아해서 그러는 게 아니라 승진시켜줄까 해서 그런대요.
글쎄, 하지만 항상 일이 그들이 생각한 대로 되는 것은 아니지.

rise. "You made some great strides this week and I'm proud of you. But it sounds like one of the things you discovered is that one of the 'main things' for a leader is to eliminate confusion. We will talk later on about confusion—which can paralyze your team—but you've taken a giant step by working with your team to figure out what the main things are in your department."

My mentor continued, obviously pleased with my report this Monday. "Something that may have contributed to the confusion on the team is a trap many managers fall into," he said. "This trap is what I call 'management land,' where things are not always as they seem. And there's something else about this place—sometimes it's difficult to escape management land.

"In management land, simple things often become complex and people easily lose perspective. Managers begin to think the games others play are what are most important."

"In management land, people are rewarded for saying only the things managers want to hear. Egos are big and it's difficult to discover the truth. Management land can be described as confusing, frustrating and sometimes comical to those on the outside."

get in touch ~와 접촉하다 **on the mark** 꼭 들어맞는 **get away with** 빠져 나가다, 모면하다 **keep piling with work** 더 많은 일을 계속 넘기다 **beaten down** (구어체)몹시 지친, 지쳐 빠진

· · ·

Let's look at it this way. '자, 이렇게 한번 보도록(생각하도록) 하지' 실제로 영어에서 this와 that은 거리로 구분되지 않고 주로 화자의 느낌에 따라 표현된 다. 일반적으로 this는 말하려고 하는 내용이나 지금 상황을, that은 말했던 내 용이나 현재상황이 아닌 것(장소도 포함)을 표현할 때 사용된다.
Those are the ones who are doing as little as they can get away with. '이들은 책임을 모면할 수 있을 정도로만 일을 하는 사람들이지'

"What you learned this week is that you have to escape from management land and get in touch with your people. Chad and Jeni were right on the mark when they said that their expectations of you were simple: hire good people, coach everyone to become better, and dehire the ones who don't pull their share of the load. Jeff, their expectations actually translate into great advice!"

"Let's look at it this way. On most teams there are three types of employees. Some are superstars—people who have the experience, knowledge and desire to be the very best at their jobs. Others are middle stars—they may not have the experience to be a superstar yet. Or maybe they are former superstars who for some reason lost their motivation to be the best. And then there are those I call falling stars. Those are the ones who are doing as little as they can get away with."

"A typical team has about 30% superstars, 50% middle stars and 20% falling stars. If you keep piling more work on your superstars—like Chad and Jeni suggested you had done—then you shouldn't expect them to continue to be superstars. Oh sure, some superstars will always be superstars regardless of the workload; but others will be beaten down into middle stars because of the additional

but others will be beaten down into middle stars because of the additional work you pile on. '하지만 다른 사람들은 당신이 쌓아둔 추가 업무 때문에 지쳐서 미들스타가 되고 말 겁니다'

work you pile on."

"Let's take a look at this chart:

"Where is the minimum acceptable level of performance

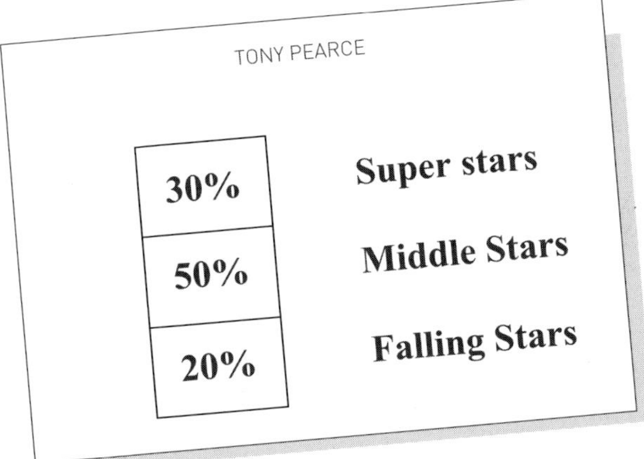

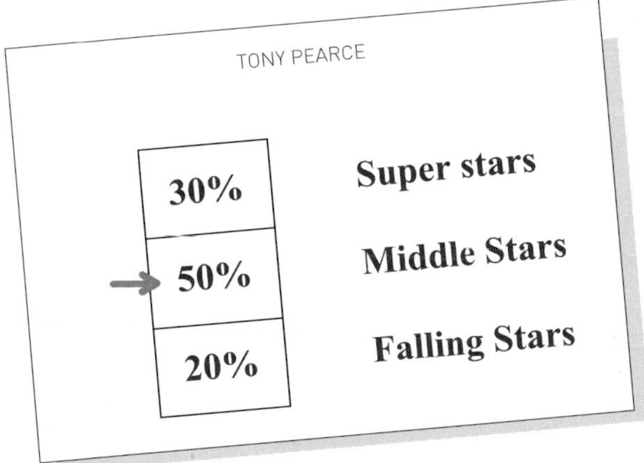

minimum acceptable level 최소 수용기준 **acknowledge someone with**
~를 알려주다, 인정하다 **decent** 엄하지 않은, 너그러운

represented on this chart?"

"Of course!" I said. "That's pretty simple. The minimum acceptable performance is in the middle of the 50%. Right here."

"No, Jeff. The minimum acceptable performance is actually here, at the bottom of the 20%," Tony corrected.

"You see, the people at the very bottom of the chart are

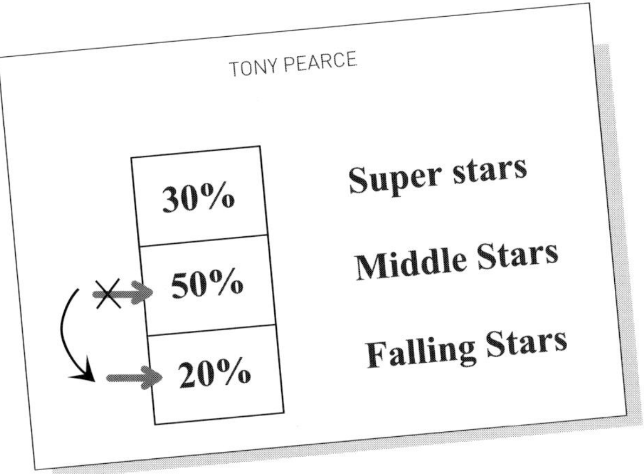

still on your team, so their behavior must be acceptable to you. In fact, many managers—and you probably know some of these people—actually reward their falling stars by giving them less work while acknowledging them with decent performance reviews!"

"When you do that, you should expect more people to

accommodating 호의적인   **emphatic about** (필요성을) 역설하다, 강조하다
retrieve 되찾다, 회수하다

. . .

Why not do less when where are still rewards? '아직 줄 포상(rewards)이
있다면 좀 줄이는 건 어떤가?

. . .

I'm telling you.
진짜라니까.

'말을 하다' 에 의미로 사용되지만 '진심임을 강조' 할 때도 사용한다. I'm
serious도 같은 의미이다.

fall into that category. Why not do less when there are still rewards?"

"Your job is not to lower the bottom by adjusting for and accommodating the lowest performing employees. You should be raising the top by recognizing and rewarding superstar behaviors!"

"You simply cannot ignore performance issues and expect your superstars to stick around for very long," Tony was emphatic about this point. "That's what Chad and Jeni were telling you. They said they needed you to coach everyone on the team and to dehire those who didn't carry their share of the load."

"I want you to try this. Write in your spiral notebook the name of each team member and then categorize them as superstars, middle stars or falling stars. And include Jeni and Chad as well."

"That's pretty easy," I said. "I definitely know my superstars and falling stars. I guess everyone else is a middle star. So, I've identified six superstars, including Jeni and Chad. Three team members are falling stars and eight are middle stars."

"Okay," said Tony. "Now I want you to take that back to your office, go to your files, and retrieve every person's

We're out of time. '시간이 다 되었군'
first, second, third, finally 처럼 글을 쓰거나 말을 논리 정연하게 정리할 때,
보는 사람이나 듣는 사람으로 하여금 내용의 구분을 쉽게 하는 말을 signal
words라 한다. 이는 비즈니스 상에서 필수적으로 사용된다.

most recent performance review. Then, put their most recent performance review score next to their name. Next, pull their personnel file. Beside each name, note each time that you've documented some kind of recognition or performance improvement over the past six months. It could be a letter of appreciation or a performance improvement document. Please bring that sheet with you next week."

"Well, once again, we're out of time, Jeff. But you're making some great progress, and I appreciate you taking our sessions seriously," Tony said with a smile. "Oh, and by the way, I am enjoying my time with you as well. So tell me, what are you going to do before we meet next week?"

"Well, I'm going to focus on several things," I began. "First, I will complete the superstars, middle stars and falling stars exercise…that may be interesting. Second, I will continue my team's discussion on identifying the 'main things' so we can begin eliminating confusion. Third, I'm going to work with human resources to start interviewing to fill the positions that are open. And finally, I'll begin the process of coaching my employees. But I need your help in this area — I'm not sure exactly how to do that."

I will be honared to help you on the coaching part. ‘나는 코칭에 대해서
자네에게 기꺼이 도움을 주겠네’

"Great! You've got some work to do. And it sounds like you've already started thinking about our next meeting. I will be honored to help you on the coaching part—we can work on that next week."

"See you next week!"

**Your job is not to lower the bottom by adjusting for and accom-
modating the lowest performing employees.** '자네의 일은 성과가 낮은 직
원들을 수용하고 그들에게 맞춰서 기준을 낮추는 것이 아니네' 여기서 lower
the bottom은 기준을 낮추는 것으로 해석할 수 있다.

GET OUT OF MANAGEMENT LAND

✓ *Get in touch with your people*

✓ *Your job is not to lower the bottom by adjusting and accommodating the falling stars. You should be raising the top by recognizing and rewarding super star behaviors.*

gabled 왜곡된 **swiftly** 신속히, 즉시 **inconsistent** 모순된

· · ·

Hoping my words were making sense and weren't as garbled as I thought they sounded. '내 말이 왜곡되게 들리지 않고 즉시 올바르게 전달되길 바라면서'

I feel like I took some quantum leaps backwards since last week. '지난 주 이후로 아주 엄청난 퇴보(후퇴)를 한 기분이에요' quantum leap은 '양자비약'이라는 물리용어이지만 여기서는 '엄청난 변화'로 이해할 수 있다.

· · ·

I hardly slept all weekend.
You look terrible. Why don't you get some sleep?
주말 내내 거의 못 잤어요.
모습이 말이 아니네. 눈 좀 붙이지 그래?

The "Do Right" Rule

I arrived at Tony's house before 8 a.m. for our fourth meeting.

"Jeff, come on in. What brings you here so early?"

"I have a major issue that I need to talk to you about, and I was hoping we could meet a little longer today," I began, hoping my words were making sense and weren't as garbled as I thought they sounded. "I've hardly slept all weekend, and I really need your advice, Tony."

"No problem. Let me get us some coffee and we can get started." Tony swiftly returned with two steaming mugs of fresh coffee, settled into his winged-back chair and said, "Okay. What's up?"

"I feel like I took some quantum leaps backward since last week," I said. "I completed the superstar, middle star, and falling star exercise and found I had been really inconsistent in how I evaluated my employees. Some of my

bottom line ‘결론’ 이라는 뜻의 관용표현 **lump into** (사람이나 사물을) 한데 묶다 **as far as** ~에 관한 한 **disgust** 혐오감 **a sip of** 한 모금

• • •

Now I was on a roll. ‘나는 불안해하고 있었다’ on a roll은 상황에 따라 다르게 해석될 수 있는데, 일반적으로 ‘승승장구하다’ 라는 의미로 쓰이다.

• • •

He doesn't want to stop playing—he's on a roll.
아마 그 친구는 여기서 멈추지 않을 거야. 승승장구하고 있잖아.

falling stars actually had better performance reviews than my superstars. I also checked the personnel files, though I already knew what was there—or should I say wasn't there. There were no letters of recognition and only one performance improvement documented over the past six months, and it was on a superstar."

"The bottom line is—I've lumped everyone into the middle as far as recognition and performance imp-rovement. No wonder Jeni and Chad felt abused!" Now I was on a roll. "Discovering what I've been doing is disgusting. I should have known better. Actually, I did know better, but I did it anyway."

I took a sip of coffee. "Then, I continued with our team discussion on identifying the main thing, and we did make some progress in that area. Finally, human resources is working on finding some candidates to interview as we try to fill those two open positions on my team."

"The other area that I committed to start working on this week was coaching. Of course, I assumed that coaching for the superstars and middle stars would be positive recognition. I guess my concept was that falling stars were the only ones where I would need to address performance issues."

dependable 믿음직스러운 **cope** 극복하다, 대처하다 **state** 명확히 제시하다
termination 해고 **to my knowledge** 내가 알기로는 **struggle** 발버둥치는,
분투하는

· · ·

here's the deal. '자, 들어보세요' 라는 의미로 본론(핵심)을 이야기하려 할 때
쓰는 표현이다.

"However, I have a major issue on my team, and it involves one of my superstars. Here's the deal: Todd has been with our company for four years. He's really good at his job and has a good relationship with all the members of our team. He is dependable, consistent and knowledgeable. But, three weeks ago I discovered that Todd has been drinking on the job. I talked to him about it, and he said that he understood it was wrong, but he was working through some personal issues and was just trying to cope as best he could."

"I told him that I understood, but using alcohol during work hours is against our company policy and our team's code of behavior. So I wrote him a warning letter stating that the next violation would lead to termination."

"Well, last Friday, I saw him drinking again. I happened to be walking by his office around two o'clock and saw him pouring some scotch into his coffee mug. I don't think Todd even saw me. I just kept walking down the hall."

"No one else knows about this situation. If HR knew, they would have already asked me to terminate him. To my knowledge, no one on the team knows about his problem. At the same time, I feel for him—I know he's struggling, and I really want to help him."

sympathetic 동정적인, 인정 있는 **gut wrench** (장이 비틀어짐을 느낄 정도로) 고통스러운 **potential consequence** (그와 관계된) 가능한 결과 **reasonable and fair** 합리적이고 공정한 **caught** 들키다, 걸리다(일반적으로 get caught로 표현한다)

· · ·

I remembered what you said about raising the top and not lowering the bottom. '나는 당신이 기준을 낮추는 것이 아니라 높이는 것에 대해 말한 것을 기억한다' 여기서 기준이란 직원들의 업무 능력에 대한 기준을 말한다.

· · ·

Last week we went over budget, so this year we need to cut corners. Yea, These types of decisions are gut wrenching.
지난주에 예산을 검토해봤는데 올해에는 (인원)삭감이 필요할 것 같네.
그래, 이런 종류의 결정을 하기란 매우 고통스러운 일이지.

"Also, I remembered what you said about raising the top and not lowering the bottom. If I let him go, then I would have three open positions, and I would have lost another one of my superstars, which doesn't help my situation."

"What I think I want to do is to 'forget' what I saw Friday and just watch to see if he does it again. What do you think, Tony?"

My mentor's voice was sympathetic. "I understand where you're coming from, Jeff. I've been there, too. These types of decisions are gut wrenching. And, no, I'm not going to tell you what to do. This must be your decision. However I am going to ask you some questions that may help with your decision-making process."

"First, does Todd understand the company policy and your team's code of behavior about drinking on the job?"

"Yes," I nodded. "In fact, we discussed it in detail in our performance counseling three weeks ago, and he had to sign a document stating he clearly understood the policy as well as the potential consequence."

"Are the policy and your expectations reasonable and fair?" Tony asked.

"Yes, I believe so," I answered.

"So what if one of your falling stars was caught drinking

empathetic (감정을) 이해하는 pay the price 대가를 치르다 convenience
편의, 편리

· · ·

That does not appeal to me. '그건 저에게 와 닿지 않아요'
It sounds to me as though you're using that statement to justify not
doing the right thing. '그 발언은 마치 자네가 옳은 일을 하지 않는 것을 정
당화하려고 하는 말처럼 들린다네'

on the job?"

"That's easy," I said. "I would dehire him and move forward. But this is not so easy. Todd is having personal problems, and he's one of my few superstars…and besides, I'd be lowering the top, not raising the bottom!"

Tony paused before his next question. "So, what is the right thing to do?"

"I really don't know," I responded. "I want to be empathetic and help him, but I know he broke the rules. The right thing to do, probably, is let him go. But I would be the one paying the price to do the right thing because then I would have another open position and one less superstar. Frankly, that does not appeal to me."

"Okay, Jeff. Let's think about this from a couple of different perspectives. First, you've mentioned several times that you would be lowering the top if you let Todd go. I don't agree with you. It sounds to me as though you're using that statement to justify not doing the right thing."

"And before you say anything, let me explain. Your job is to raise the top for long-term, sustained success, not for shor-term convenience. Short-term results are easy. You can threaten people, pay them more, or just give them what they want, and you can get short-term results."

establish 수립(제정)하다 **criteria** 목록, 기준서 **its obvious that** ~는 명백한 일이다 **address the issue** 문제를 처리하다 **subscribe to (something)** (의견 등에) 동의하다

· · ·

It requires delivering the consequences—both positive and negative—based on decisions that employees make. '긍정적이든 부정적이든 직원들이 내린 결정에 근거한 내용(결과)을 이행을 해야 한다' 여기서 deliver는 여기서 '이행하다' 의 뜻으로 쓰였다.

Do what is right even when no one is watching. '아무도 지켜보지 않더라도 바른 것을 행하라'

"Achieving long-term results is much more difficult. It requires establishing a code of behavior that must be followed. It requires providing accurate feedback. It requires delivering the consequences—both positive and negative—based on decisions that employees make. All of these require courage on your part to do the right thing."

"People can be superstars in one area and falling stars in another area. You've categorized Todd as a superstar based on your performance criteria. However it's obvious that he's a falling star based on your code of behavior. So you need to address this issue as though he's a falling star because that's what he is in this area."

"Second, I subscribe to the 'do right rule.' Simply stated, do what is right even when no one is watching! Of course, doing the right thing isn't always easy—in fact sometimes it's real hard—but just remember that doing the right thing is always right.

"Now if you don't have a code of behavior or performance expectations, it's difficult to know what is right. In this case, that's not a problem…at least it doesn't appear to be a problem, based on what you've said.

"Sometimes it's difficult to know what is 'right' when you're in the middle of a crisis like you are right now with

evaluate 평가하다 **alternatives** 대안 **conceivable problem** 예상될 수 있는 문제 **simulated** 모의(실험)훈련된 **contingency** 우발사건, 뜻밖의 사고 **cockpit** (비행기, 우주선 등의) 조정실 **go wrong** 잘못되다 **hydraulic problem** 유압장치상의 문제 **implement** 이행하다 **procedure** 절차 **point out** 지적하다 **from time to time** 때때로 **altitude** 고도

this situation. I have found that the best decisions are normally made before you're in a crisis. You can think more clearly and evaluate alternatives better."

"I learned this from a friend of mine who is a pilot. He once told me that every conceivable problem that could happen while he was flying the plane had been simulated, documented, and placed in a contingency manual in the cockpit. That manual documents everything that can go wrong and what actions to take if there's a problem."

"You see, pilots don't make decisions when they're in a crisis—they implement plans that were made before the crisis. For example, if a light is flashing, signaling that there's a hydraulic problem on the aircraft, the pilot opens the manual and finds the procedure for correcting the problem. Then he implements that procedure."

"It would be difficult for a pilot to think of everything he might need to do while he's in a crisis and the plane is losing altitude," he pointed out.

"In business, from time to time we see lights flashing, indicating we have a problem. When that happens, some managers will throw a rug over the light so they can't see it flashing—in other words, they ignore it. Sure, they may feel better, but the company is still losing altitude."

unscrew bulb 전구를(돌려) 빼내다 **gauge** 게이지(계기판) **smash** 때려부수다 **temporarily** 일시적으로 **decide upon** ~으로 결정하다 **go away** 가버리다 **resolve** 해결하다 **Confucius** 공자 **cowardice** 비겁한 **discipline** 원칙 **commitment** (약속을 지키는)책임

· · ·

Your vision is cloudy. '당신의 판단력이 흐려진다'

· · ·

I work six days a week, but I only earn chicken feed. I need to find another job.
Hey, I think your vision is cloudy just because money. Your job has a vision.
난 일주일에 6일을 일하고도 쥐꼬리만큼 밖에 못 벌어. 아무래도 다른 일을 알아봐야 할 것 같아.
이봐, 돈 때문에 잠시 잊은 것 같은데. 네 일은 비전이 있잖아.

"Other managers may unscrew the bulb...no more annoying light flashing. But when they check the other business gages, the company is still losing altitude."

"Some may smash the light with a hammer. They may feel better temporarily, but the company is still going down."

"The only way to fix the problem is to go directly to what's causing the light to flash and fix the problem. Like the pilot, an action plan should have been decided upon long before the crisis developed."

"If you think about it, you're in the middle of a crisis right now — lights are flashing — and your vision is cloudy. Sure, it's easy to justify going down the least painful path and ignoring the problem instead of doing what is right. But the truth is the problem won't just go away. You have to take action — you have to do what is right and resolve the issue."

"I read where Confucius once said, 'To know what is right and not do it is the worst cowardice.' It sounds as though even Confucius subscribed to the 'do right rule.' But actually living the 'do right rule' is tough because it requires discipline, commitment and courage. Think about it..."

ethnic department 윤리(도덕성을 총괄하는) 부서 **compliance officer** 규범
(준법을 관리하는) 간부 **integrity** 청렴

• • •

The closer you are to the situation, the more you can see. '상황에 근접
하면 할수록 좀 더 많은 것을 볼 수 있게 된다네'
Everything counts when it comes to your leadership. '리더십과 관련해
서는 모든 것이 중요하다' 여기서 count는 '중요하다' 라는 의미로 쓰였다.

"My third question, Jeff, is why do you think you're the only one seeing the problem? Many times the manager is the last to know about a problem on the team. What the manager sees is normally a very small part of the whole. It's like an iceberg in the ocean. Above the water you can see the tip, but what lies below is much larger, much more powerful, and usually, much more destructive."

"The closer you are to the situation, the more you can see. Todd's teammates are closer to this 'iceberg' than you are, and I would be surprised if they're not wondering why you are allowing Todd to do what he's doing."

"Fourth, EVERYTHING counts when it comes to your leadership. If you think ignoring the problem doesn't matter, you're wrong—you're always leading, even when you're ignoring a problem. Your team doesn't really care if your company has an ethics department or compliance officer. What matters to your team is what you do. And, everything you do matters because your team is watching…and depending on you to do the right thing."

"Ignoring issues puts your own integrity at risk. And if you lose your integrity, you won't be able to develop or maintain trust, the very basis for relationships. Jeff, I can't say this enough: You must guard your integrity as if it's

go through (길이나 장애물을)헤쳐 나가다 **aware of** ~을 알고 있는

• • •

I can't say this enough. '이건 더 말할 나위도 없습니다' 말하려는 내용을 강조할 때 자주 쓰이는 표현이다.
That is what it is. '원래 그런 거라구' 사실이나 내용을 강조할 때 사용되는 표현이다.

your most precious leadership possession, because that is what it is. But you are the leader here and the choice is yours."

"Obviously, you have a decision to make. So what are you going to do?"

Tony's message was clear but difficult at the same time. "Okay, I know everything you said is probably correct," I began. "But, it's hard to do what is right when the pressure is on. I'm not looking forward to three open positions, one less superstar—at least in most areas—and facing Todd, knowing he's going through some personal issues. It's tough."

"But, I know I've been fair…and I know he made the choice to put his employment at risk. And I guess you're right—I'm probably not the only person aware of the issue. I think others on the team are watching me and judging me on how I handle this situation."

"I'll go to human resources as soon as I get back to the office, and I'll get their help in working my way though this issue."

I took another deep breath. "Well, Tony. It probably won't surprise you that I already see a place where I need some help from you next week. You mentioned we would

cover ~대하여 다루다, 이야기하다 **in the meantime** 그러는 동안에 **look forward to ~ing** ~하기를 고대하다, 기대하다

· · ·

I've got to make some good hiring decisions··· '영어에서 ~해야 한다' 의 표현은 have to, should, must, have got to 등이 있다. '해야 한다' 는 의지를 갖는 주체가 누구냐에 따라 다르게 사용되는데, have to는 주어에 의지에 따라, should는 주이가 아닌 상황의 의지에 따라, must는 어느 쪽에 상관없이 가장 강한 어감을, have got to는 have to와 같은 어감을 갖는 표현이다.

· · ·

I'm between jobs. I am still looking for work.
You will get it soon. Good luck.
일을 못 잡았어. 아직도 직장을 구하러 다니고 있다니까.
곧 생기겠지. 행운을 빌어.

between jobs는 실직된 상태를 뜻하는 표현이다.

discuss hiring at one of these sessions...I think I need to do that pretty fast. Can we do it next week? I've got to make some good hiring decisions—especially now. Wish me luck."

"Good luck this week, Jeff. And we'll plan to cover hiring next week," Tony said. "In the meantime, you'll be fine as you work through this issue. Look at it this way. It's a temporary problem—a temporary problem you have to face. I look forward to hearing about it next week."

Guard your integrity like it's your most precious management possession. '청렴을 가장 소중한 경영의 재산인 것처럼 지켜라'

DO THE RIGHT THING

✓ *Develop your action plan before you get into a crisis.*

✓ *Guard your integrity like it's your most precious management possession.*

be tempted to do something ~을 하고 싶어 하다 **role-playing** 역할극(다른 사람의 입장에서 행동해보는 것) **be about to** ~하기 바로 직전에 **witness** 목격하다(목격자) **termination session** 해고과정(해고를 위한 면담과정) **compute** 신정(계산)하다 **payroll** 급료 지불 명부(지불 급료 총액을 말하기도 한다) **check** 수표(미국에선 반드시 급여를 수표로 지불하게 되어 있다)

• • •

I held myself back. ‘나는 내 자신을 자제했다’ hold someone(something) back은 ‘억누르다’, ‘자제하다’ 라는 의미로 hold 대신에 keep을 더 자주 사용한다.

So, fill me in. ‘자 그러니 말해보게’ fill something(someone) in은 ‘~에 무엇인가를 채워(끼워)넣다’ 라는 뜻으로 여기서는 ‘그 이야기에 나를 넣어 달라’ 즉 ‘그 이야기를 해 달라’ 로 해석할 수 있다.

The Fifth Monday_

Hire Tough

As I drove up to Tony's house, I could see him at the door.

"Hello, Jeff," he waved. "I'm the one who could hardly wait for you to come this week. In fact, I was tempted to call you several times to find out how your week was going, but I held myself back. So, fill me in."

"Well, it was an interesting week to say the least," I began. "I left here and went straight to Kim in human resources to discuss the Todd issue. She asked me some of the same questions you did, and we decided I didn't have a choice—I had to terminate Todd for drinking on the job."

"So, Kim and I began 'role-playing' the discussion I was about to have with Todd. And, Tony, the role-play helped me feel more prepared and confident. I also asked Kim to witness the termination session. We computed his final pay, got payroll to cut the check, and called him into

self-respect 자존심 **dignity** 존엄(성) **firm and fair with** ~에 단호하고 공정
하게 **stunned** (놀람으로)어안이 벙벙해진, 아연실색한 **something 'as
minor as this'** 이처럼 사소한(별것 아닌) 일 **accuse** 비난하다 **compassion**
동정, 연민 **anticipate** 예상하다 **have no heart** 동정하지 않는, 인정머리 없
는 **extenuate** 정상을 참작하다

. . .

We were only implementing his decision. '우리는 단지 그의 결정을 이행
하는 것뿐입니다'

the conference room."

"Kim's advice to me before the session was that we needed to do everything we could to maintain Todd's self-respect and dignity, while being firm and fair with him."

"When Todd walked into the room, he obviously knew something was up. I asked him to sit down and began talking to him about the drinking problem. He was stunned that I would terminate him for something 'as minor as this.' He also accused me of not having any compassion because he was going through some personal problems. He then went on to say that the team wouldn't survive without him because he was more the leader of the team than I was."

"Thankfully, Kim and I had anticipated and role-played all of his reactions. She said the majority of people who are fired feel the same way: It's someone else's fault, 'management has no heart,' and there are extenuating circumstances. I must admit that she did a great job in preparing me for the meeting. Her last advice before the meeting was to remember that Todd chose to fire himself—we were only implementing his decision. That thought made me feel a little better."

"Anyway, the meeting was 30 extremely long minutes of

intense 강렬한, 격렬한 debate with ~와 논쟁하다 clear out 정리하다
take up the slack 느슨함을 죄다, 기강을 바로잡다 overhear 우연히 듣다,
엿듣다 cover up ~의 실수를 감싸다 finalize 완성하다, 끝내다

· · ·

The meeting was 30 extremely long minutes of intense emotions. '그 미
팅은 격한 감정으로 30분이라는 아주 긴 시간 동안 진행되었다'

intense emotions. I really felt badly for Todd, but kept remembering I was only implementing his decision. Finally, he understood we weren't going to debate with him, so he took his check, cleared out his desk and left."

"After taking a few minutes to steady my own emotions, it was then time for my weekly team meeting. Of course, the first thing everyone wanted to know was what happened to Todd. He had left without saying anything, but they saw him clean out his desk. I told them that Todd was no longer with our company and that my number one priority was to fill his position as soon as possible. They asked what happened, and I followed Kim's advice, again, saying I would not go into any details other than we have to work together to take up the slack we all feel without Todd."

"Here was my surprise: I overheard two of my middle stars saying they were relieved they wouldn't have to cover up for Todd's drinking any longer. I don't know if I was the last to discover Todd drinking on the job, but I do know I wasn't the only person aware of the problem. My team was watching and my integrity was being challenged. Tony, you were right again."

"The rest of the meeting went well. We finalized what

come up with ~를 제안하다 **logistical issues** (결원으로 인한 업무상의)배치 문제 **be anxious(eager) to** (간절히) ~하고 싶어 하다

• • •

all in all '대체적으로' in all 과 all in all은 거의 비슷하게 해석되지만 약간의 차이가 있다. cf)In all, there were 28 people there. '다 합쳐 28명의 사람이 있었다'
I should have involved Kim in human resources without hesitation. '주 저 없이(당연히) 인사부에 킴을 관여시켜야 했었다'

the main things were for us to accomplish. Here are the three main things we came up with:

1. Treat each person on our team with dignity and respect.
2. Deliver outstanding service to our customers.
3. Provide profits to our company.

"Sound familiar? Almost the same as the main things you told me in our first meeting. I told the team they will be asked, every day, what are the main things. I also told them that if what they were being asked to do by someone else didn't fall into these three areas, they had the right to say no—regardless of who asked."

"So all in all, the week was not too bad. Losing Todd created some logistical issues, but we worked our way through them. I also learned I should have involved Kim in human resources without hesitation. She knows her stuff and wants to help me. In the meantime, she has identified 20 candidates for me to interview for my three open positions. I have interviews scheduled on Wednesday, Thursday and Friday of this week, and I want to fill these positions by the weekend. So I'm anxious to hear what you have to say about hiring."

Now it was Tony's turn to talk. "Great. I'm glad eve-

worked out (일이)잘 해결되다, 풀리다 **asset** 자산

• • •

Congratulate me. I just got bumped up to vice president!
Wow, I'm so proud of you.
축하해주세요. 저 방금 부사장으로 승진했어요.
와! 네가 정말 자랑스럽구나.

be proud of는 상대의 일이나 행위에 대한 큰 찬사의 표현으로 사용된다.
'You made it!' 혹은 'You are there!!' 라고 표현할 수도 있다.

rything worked out with the Todd situation. Jeff, you did the right thing, even though it was tough. I'm proud of you."

"With respect to the hiring, let's start with a question: What is the most valuable asset in your company?"

"That's easy," I said. "People are the most important resource in any company. The people make the company."

"Okay. Now, what is the greatest liability of your company?"

This question was more difficult. "Hmm. I would think that something like product failure would be our greatest liability."

"Well, I don't agree with you on either point," Tony responded.

"I'm not sure I'm right about the greatest liability," I defended, "but I know I'm right about people being the most important asset in our company. How could you argue that? Customers judge our company on the people they deal with. So, people are the most important asset."

"I agree with everything you said—the question was a trick question," Tony admitted. "The most important asset in your company is having the RIGHT PEOPLE on your team. If you have the right people on your team you have a

liability 부담, 손실 **ineffective** 무능한, 쓸모없는 **make-up** (여기서는 팀의) 구성 **diversity** 다양성, 변화 **spark** 불을 지피다 **hire tough** 까다롭게 채용하는 **privilege** 명예, 특권 **earn one's way** 해내다, 이뤄내다 **it will be a whole lot easier to** ~하기가 훨씬 더 용이해지다

· · ·

Make it a privilege for someone to earn his or her way on your team.
'사람들로 하여금 너의 팀에 들어오는 것을 특권이라고 생각하게 만들어라'

· · ·

Instead of negotiating directly with the client, let's find a go-between who is completely impartial.
I don't think that is reasonable. We have to spend extra money.
고객과 직접 협상하지 말고 완전히 중립적 입장에 있는 협상가를 찾아보는 건 어떨까?
그건 합리적인 것 같지 않아. 추가비용이 들잖아.

go-between은 협상가(negotiator)를 의미한다. I think는 '~인 것 같다' 라는 구어체적인 표현이다. 따라서 I don't think는 '~이 아닌 것 같아' 로 해석할 수 있다.

great chance to be successful."

"The greatest liability in your company could be having the WRONG PEOPLE on your team. In fact, there is nothing any competitor can do to hurt your team as much as having the wrong person on the team."

"The most important thing you do as a leader is to hire the right people. You cannot have a strong and effective team with weak and ineffective people."

"Jeff, you have a great opportunity right now. With three open positions, you can make a big difference in the make-up of your team. You can add some diversity, generate new ideas, and add some energy and spark by picking the right people to join your team."

"You said that you wanted to hire these three people by the weekend," he continued. "I don't think that is reasonable. Your job is to hire tough—make it a privilege for someone to earn his or her way on your team. If you hire tough, it will be a whole lot easier to manage the RIGHT PEOPLE."

"The decision you have to make is to hire tough and manage easy, or hire easy and manage tough. I can assure you that the best thing to do is to take your time on the front end so that you can enjoy having the RIGHT

up front 먼저, 우선적으로 **candidate** 지원자 **in advance** 미리, 앞서서
figure out 해결하다 **emotionally involved** 감정이 개입된 **better off** 한결
더 (일이) 잘되다

· · ·

it's not a poor reflection on you. '자네 능력(의견)을 비하하는 건 아니네'
reflection이 대상을 표현하는 on(upon)과 함께 쓰이면 '~에 대한 비난, 비방,
문책' 등을 의미한다.

PEOPLE on your team."

"When you begin the process of interviewing and hiring, understand up front that you are probably not a great interviewer. Don't take that personally—it's not a poor reflection on you. It's just that you don't use your interviewing skills very often. If you don't use the skills very often, you need a good system to help you make the best decision. I'm sure that Kim in HR will provide you with an interviewing track to follow. And you may even want to ask her to participate in the hiring process with you."

"The first mistake some people make in interviewing is lack of preparation. You shouldn't begin preparing for the interview when the candidate is in the lobby. Is that the way you want to treat someone who may become your most valuable asset? Every question should be prepared in advance so you spend your time listening and evaluating instead of trying to figure out what question you want to ask next."

"Another problem with interviewing is you're always emotionally involved. The open position is taking time and energy away from you, so you want to fill the job fast. Fight those emotions. You will be far better off by taking your time and getting the right person. I suggest you ask

narrow down 좁히다, 요약하다 **insight on**(into) ~에 대한 통찰

Kim or someone in HR to help—they're not faced with the same emotions you have about these openings.

"The Three Rules of Three in hiring are: interview at least three qualified candidates for every position; interview the candidates three times; and have three people evaluate the candidates. I know that sounds like a long process, but remember—your job is to hire tough."

"Kim has already provided you with 20 qualified candidates for the three positions. That's good. You have more choices. After the initial interviews, narrow the field down to your best nine candidates. I would schedule interviews with those nine candidates at times that are different than their original interview time. In other words, if your initial interview was in the morning with one person, interview them the next time in the afternoon or evening. You'll be working with them all day, so why not see what they're like at different times of the day?"

"Since you and Kim are involved in the process, you may want to allow one of your superstars to be involved as well. The superstar may be able to give you some insight on how the candidate would fit with your current team."

"If there is any question whether a person is qualified or not, pass on them and keep searching for the right person.

time is up(시작할 또는 마칠)시간이 되다 **enthusiasm** 열의, 의욕

Never lower your standards just to fill a position! You'll pay for it later."

"I see that our time is up for today. So tell me, what are you going to do differently during this coming week?"

"Well, first I'm going to slow down the hiring process and do it right. My goal is to hire tough and make it an honor for someone to be on our team. Next, I'm going to involve Kim and one of my superstars in the process—and I will follow the Three Rules of Three so that I have enough information to make a great decision."

"I know this is the most important decision I'll make, and I'm going to do my very best to make a great decision," I finished, thinking of how much information Tony had shared that I could use right away."

"You're a good student, Jeff, and I can feel your enthusiasm about your opportunity to bring some new people to your team. Hire tough!"

"See you next week!"

**Mr. Silver, you're out of order! If you speak again without permission,
I'm going to be forced to ask you to leave.
Ok. But you will pay for it later.**
실버씨, 규정위반입니다. 한 번 더 승인 없이 발언한다면 퇴장시킬 수밖에 없
습니다.
좋습니다. 그러나 후에 대가를 치르게 될 거예요.

HIRE TOUGH

✓ *The most important asset in your company is having the RIGHT PEOPLE on your team.*

✓ *Never lower your standards just to fill a position! You will pay for it later.*

pull into (차량 등이)안으로 들어가다 **taxing** 부담스러운, 고생스러운

Do Less or Work Faster

By this time, I so looked forward to my Monday Mornings with Tony, that I was getting up much earlier…and feeling much better about so many aspects of what had once been such a disaster area, both at work and at home.

I pulled into Tony's driveway well before our meeting time, but when I rang the bell, Tony appeared, as charming as always. "Good morning, Jeff," he said. "How are things going? Did you make any progress filling your open positions?"

"Yes, I made some real progress, Tony. Kim and I interviewed all 20 candidates for the three open positions. It was pretty taxing, but Kim provided me with a good process to follow, and we have narrowed the 20 down to nine possible candidates. The final round of interviews are scheduled for Wednesday, Thursday, and Friday this week.

time consuming 시간이 걸리는 **things outside my control** 내 능력 밖에 일들 **harsh** 거친, 잔인한 **counter** 맞서다, 대항하다 **defensively** 방어적으로 **have control over** ~을 관리(제어)하고 있다 **come across** (꾸짖는 듯)말하다

· · ·

I've hardly done anything else. ‘다른 일은 거의 아무 것도 할 수 없었어요’
Aren't you being a little harsh? ‘좀 심하신 것 아닌가요?’ 이외에도 상대의 말이나 행위가 정도를 넘었을 때 사용하는 일반적인 표현으로 ‘you are too much’ 가 있다.
I'm trying to make a point. ‘나는 요점을 명확히 하려는 서예요’

· · ·

We're not going to make our goal unless we skip some lunches and really knuckle down.
I understand but Woe is me.
점심을 거르면서 일을 정말 열심히 해야 해, 그렇지 많으면 목표에 닿을 수 없어.
이해는 하지만 너무 힘들어요.

woe is me는 ‘괴롭다’ 혹은 ‘슬프다’ 를 의미하는 관용표현이다.

By our next meeting I should have offered the jobs to the three best candidates."

"And I'll tell you—after our conversation last week, I'm taking the hiring process much more seriously," I confessed.

"But this hiring process has been so time consuming, I've hardly done anything else. And that's another issue I wanted your insights on—how do I get everything done?"

"Even though I feel I've made a lot of progress during our sessions, it seems my time continues to be consumed by things outside my control. It's frustrating because I want to spend more time with my team…and my family."

"Jeff, you sound the same as you did in our first meeting: 'Woe is me…I have no control over my time.' Well it sounds to me like you may be blaming your personal time management problem on things outside your control. Let me ask you this: Who can spend your time but you?"

"Aren't you being a little harsh?" I countered, defensively. "I simply said I seem to be consumed by things I feel I don't have much control over, and so I' m not able to do the important things I need—and want—to do."

"Sorry if I came across harshly," Tony apologized. "I'm trying to make a point: Your time is your responsibility. If

pastime (기분전환, 즐거운)취미, 오락 **magic bullets** 마법 탄환(어떤 문제의 해
결책이라는 의미로 사용된다) **increment** 증가, 증대

• • •

**I've discovered that there are no magic bullets when it comes to time
management.** '나는 시간운영에 관해서는 해결책을 발견하지 못했어요'

you aren't able to do the important things, only you can solve that problem. Your team is depending on you to be there for them, and that includes solving your personal problems."

"One of the major sources of stress, anxiety, and unhappiness comes from feeling like your life is out of control. You need to figure out ways to take control of your time so that you can take control of your life."

"Of course, there are some things we can't change about the way we spend our time. We have to wait in lines, at red lights, for elevators, and things like that. There's not much we can do about those things. However there is a lot we can do about situations at work."

"Jeff, I've studied time management for years—in fact it's one of my favorite pastimes—and I've discovered that there are no magic bullets when it comes to time management. I've never found anyone who had two or three hours a day they could save by doing one thing better. But, I have seen many people find an hour or two a day they could use better by doing a few things differently."

"If you want to make better use of your time, you need to be looking for the small increments of time...a minute here, five minutes there, etc. Add them all up and you'll

seldom 드물게, 좀처럼 ~않는 **myth** 신화, 오해

• • •

There's a myth out there no one seems to recognize… '사람들이 인식하지 못하는 사실이 있는데…'
That's the question we need to address. '이것이 우리가 다루어야 할 문제입니다' 여기서 address는 '다루다', '처리하다' 의 의미로 쓰였다.

create more time for you to use."

"I have also found that the job seldom overworks the person, but people often overwork themselves by making bad time management decisions. The bottom line is that most people can't solve their time problem by working harder. Doing the wrong thing harder doesn't help. What we need to do is to find ways to shorten tasks, eliminate some steps, combine some tasks, and work easier while getting things done."

"There's a myth out there no one seems to recognize, and it's this: No one can save time…we all have the same amount, and we can't carry any time over to the next day. So since we can't save time, we have to make better decisions on how we spend our time."

"I only know of two ways to spend time better. You can do less or you can do things faster. Those are our only choices. Of course there are some things we could eliminate and just say no to. But for today's session, let's say that the only option we have is to work faster. So how can you work faster? That's the question we need to add-ress."

"The first thing you need to figure out is where your time is currently going. If you want to make impro-

facilitate 용이하게(효율적으로) 하다 **categorize into** ~으로 분류하다

• • •

The first thing you need to figure out is where your time is currently going. '당신은 우선 현재 시간을 어디에 사용하고 있는지 알아봐야 한다'

vements, you've got to know what to improve. To find the answer, I suggest you track your time for two weeks so you can make some educated decisions about what to improve."

"You will find that your time is taken by the things we do and how we do things. Follow me on this: We spend our time doing the main things or doing the wrong things…and we spend our time doing things right or doing things wrong."

"For example, here's a chart showing the four choices of how we can spend our time in a meeting:

"Everything we do can be categorized into one of those

How We Do the Things We Do		
The Things We Do	**Main Things Right** Example: Run a productive and necessary meeting.	**Main Things Wrong** Example: Waste two hours during an important meeting.
	Wrong Things Right Example: Facilitate a great meeting that was not necessary.	**Wrong Things Wrong** Example: Waste everyone's time at an unnecessary meeting.

classify 분류하다   **prioritizing** 우선순위를 매김   **organizing** 구성(정리)
interruption 중단, 방해   **pareto principle** 파레토 법칙   **payoff** 수익   **yield**
(이익 등을)낳다, 가져오다

• • •

one of these(those) 일반적으로 '~중 하나' 라고 해석해도 무관하나 '~와 같
은 부류의' 라는 의미도 갖는다. ex)He is one of those quiet people. '그 사
람은 좀 조용한 부류이다'

four choices. If you keep track for two weeks, you'll know what you can do to make some better decisions. You've already identified the main things in your department. Now, classify your activities—are you doing those main things and how well are you doing them?"

"Most executives have three areas where they can make changes that will lead to major time improvements: prioritizing/organizing, interruptions, and meetings."

"While preparing for our session, I gathered some of the best tips I've found about managing my time in each of those areas. Let's talk about **prioritizing and organizing** first."

"You've probably heard of the Pareto Principle that states that 80% of your results will come from 20% of your activities. An Italian economist named Alfredo Pareto discovered the principle in the 1800's when he observed that 20% of the people in Italy controlled 80% of the wealth. Then he began looking around and discovered that the 80/20 rule applied to many things. And the Pareto Principle definitely applies to time management. It's your responsibility to yourself and your team to know where your highest payoff activities are and eliminate as many as you can of the ones that yield few results."

guru 전문가, 권위자 **shuffle** ~을 뒤섞다 **set(put) aside** 챙겨 놓다, 확보하다
return 보상, 보답 **audit** 심사, 검사 **in-box** 미결 서류함 **line item** 단순한
품목 **off a report** 보고서(형태)가 아닌 **originator** 작성자 **don't fool
yourself into**⋯ ~하는 우를 범하지 마라 **clutter** 어지르다

• • •

Touch paper only once. ‘서류(일)는 한 번에 처리하라’
Set aside some uninterrupted planning time every day. ‘매일 방해 받지
않고 계획할 수 있는 시간을 확보해라’

• • •

**If you plan on finishing your assignment before you leave on vacation,
you'd better get cracking.**
I know and I will conduct an audit on every report that hits my in-box.
휴가 전에 담당업무를 끝내려면 바로 일을 시작해야 할 걸세.
알고 있습니다. 그리고 미결 서류함의 모든 보고서를 처리하겠습니다.

"Every time management guru will tell you to **touch paper only once.** The key to paper management is to keep the paper moving: Throw it away, act upon it, or put it into your reading pile. It may not be reasonable to only touch paper once in every situation, but remember — shuffling and reshuffling paper from pile to pile with no evaluation or action is wasting your time."

"One of the most important personal tips for me is to **set aside some uninterrupted planning time every day.** It was difficult for me to discipline myself to do this, but I found that spending 20 uninterrupted minutes planning would yield the same results as 60 minutes of interrupted time. If you can't set aside 20 minutes, set aside 10. That's still a great return on your time investment."

"**Conduct an audit on every report that hits your in-box.** Is the report really necessary? If not, eliminate it. If you only need a line item off a report, ask the originator of the report to eliminate the report and send you the line item."

"**Clean your desk.** I think you should always be able to see the majority of the top of your desk. Don't fool yo-urself into thinking that a cluttered desk makes you look important. A cluttered desk makes you look disorganized

contribute to ~에 기여하다　**batch activities** 일괄처리(행동)　**batch** 일괄(처리되는 job의 묶음)　**at one sitting** 그 자리에서 바로　**deli** DELICATESSEN의 준말, 조그만 상점으로 주로 뉴욕과 같은 큰 도시에서 간단히 식사할 수 있는 곳을 의미한다.

and contributes to the shuffling and reshuffling game."

"**Control your email deliveries.** You don't go to your mailbox every 30 minutes, do you? I receive a lot of emails every day—I could be at my computer all day just responding to emails. Instead, I work my email deliveries into my personal schedule so that emails don't control my day".

"**Batch activities—do like activities together—so that you're not starting and stopping all the time.** Do all your voice mails at once. Return all phone calls at one time. Write memos or letters at one sitting. Eliminate as many transitions from one activity to another as possible."

"Here's a simple one that can give you ten, maybe fifteen minutes every day. **Go to lunch at 11 or 1.** Why everyone decides to go to lunch at noon is a mystery to me. They wait on the elevator, wait in line at the deli, wait in line to get back on the elevator, and then complain about not having enough time for lunch."

"Now let's talk about another key area of time management—**interruptions.**"

"Most people don't know who is interrupting them or why they're being interrupted. **Keep track of who is interrupting you and why they're interrupting you.**

proportion (~에 대한) 비율 **rather than** ~하기 보나는 **flow of traffic** 교통의 흐름, 혼잡한 지역

• • •

The length of the interruption is in direct proportion to the comfort level of the interrupter. '방해하는 사람의 편안함은 방해 당하는 시간과 정비례한다' 즉 '방해하는 사람이 편안할수록 방해 당하는 시간은 길어진다' 는 뜻이다.

Arrange your furniture so that your desk doesn't face the flow of traffic. '사람들이 자주 왕래하는 쪽을 마주보지 않도록 가구들을 배치하라'

Then you can make some informed decisions about how you're going to address the problem."

"I have found that **even if you can't eliminate the interruption—you can keep it short.** A general rule is this: The length of the interruption is in direct proportion to the comfort level of the interrupter. Don't let the interrupter sit down and get comfortable in your office. When someone comes into your office, stand up. You can take care of business standing up more quickly than—and just as well as—sitting down."

"Your furniture can even invite interruptions and steal some time from you. I suggest you **arrange your furniture so that your desk doesn't face the flow of traffic.** If you're looking at every person who walks down the hall, you'll be wasting a lot of time."

"**Schedule one-on-one sessions with your staff and boss** so that you can get as much as possible accomplished at one time. Gather everything you need to talk about and take care of it at one sitting rather than interrupting each other the minute something comes up."

"You may want to **ask your team: 'What do I do that wastes your time and hinders your performance?'** Some of their suggestions may surprise you and could save

gazillion zillion에서 ga를 붙여 엄청나게 많은 수를 의미 **unproductive** 비
생산적인 **fall into** ~에 빠지다 **perpetually** 지속되는, 영구히 **rush
through** 급히(날치기로) 통과시키다 **recap** (언급했던 내용을)다시 요약하다
tardy 늦은, 뒤늦은

• • •

Don't fall into the 'perpetually scheduled meeting' syndrome. '정기회
의 신드롬에 빠지지 마라'

158

you and your team valuable time."

"Finally, let's talk about one of the biggest time wasters I know of—**meetings.**"

"Jeff, I've been to a gazillion meetings in my day and have found that—if everyone is prepared, on-time and focused—most meetings can be accomplished in half the time the meeting is currently taking. The average person wastes about 250 hours per year in unproductive meetings. That's a lot of time and money being wasted! **Make your meetings productive but short.**"

"**Don't fall into the 'perpetually scheduled meeting' syndrome** where you're having meetings just because meetings are regularly scheduled. Make sure every meeting is absolutely necessary. Routine meetings are not a good investment unless they fulfill, or move forward, your objectives."

"**Always begin a meeting by covering the most important items first.** That way you ensure that you cover what you need to accomplish, and you're not rushing through the main things."

"**When people show up late, don't recap what you've covered.** When you recap, you're rewarding the tardy person and punishing the people who were on time."

dividend 할당, 배당(여기서는 '부분' 으로 해석) **counsel** 조언

. . .

Time is up. 마칠 시간이나 시작할 시간이 다 되었을 때 일반적으로 사용된다.
Following his own counsel. '그의 조언에 따라(부합하게)'

. . .

The post office is closing in ten minutes! I need you to mail this letter ASAP.
Would you relax? I know time is up.
우체국이 10분 안에 문을 닫아! 이 편지를 빨리 보내야 해.
진정 좀 할래? 나도 시간이 다 된 거 알고 있어.

ASAP는 as soon as possible의 약자로 회화에서 많이 사용한다. 특히 FBI나 경찰들을 다룬 미국 영화의 대사에서 자주 들을 수 있다.

"Probably the simplest tip that pays the biggest dividend in meeting management is to **start and end your meetings on time.** It's disrespectful and a bad investment to start a meeting later than scheduled. You waste 30 minutes of productivity by beginning a meeting with 10 people three minutes late. Think about that."

"These are just a few ideas to help you make better use of your time. There are many more. I suggest you invest some time in reading a book on time management and look for several other areas where you can find a few extra minutes."

"Speaking of time, our time is about up for this week," said Tony, following his own counsel. "So, what are you going to do differently next week?"

"Well, I'm going to finish the hiring process," I replied. "That's the main thing of all main things this week. While you were talking, I was doing a self-check on the meetings I facilitate, and I know I can do a better job creating some additional time for my team and myself. I'm also going to track who interrupts me and the number of times that I interrupt others. I may be guilty of being the #1 interrupter to my team members. And I'm going to buy a book on time management and search for other ideas to help me

enthusiastic 열렬한, 열광적인 **energize** 격려하다 **resolve** 결정, 결심

gain control of my time and my life."

"Great, Jeff!" Tony's enthusiastic response energized my own resolve. "Try out some of those ideas. I know you'll find some more time for yourself and your family."

"See you next week!"

Look for small increments of time by prioritizing, limiting interruptions, and effectively managing meetings. '우선순위를 정하고, 방해요소를 줄이고, 효율적으로 회의를 관리하여 조금이라도 여유 시간을 늘려라'

DO LESS/WORK FASTER

✓ *Your time is your responsibility. Take control of your time so you can take control of your life.*

✓ *Look for small increments of time by prioritizing, limiting interruptions, and effectively managing meeting.*

promptly 즉시 **turn down** 거절하다

Buckets and Dippers

I arrived at Tony's promptly at 8:30 a.m. He greeted me at the door.

"Jeff, how are you today and how was your week?" he said, guiding me into the library. "Did you make any progress filling your open positions? And how about your time management? Did you find any places where you could spend your time better? And of course, I want to hear how the team is doing."

I had spent the weekend looking forward to our Monday morning conversation. "Last week was a much better week. Kim and I completed the interviewing and made job offers to the best three candidates," I said.

"Two of them accepted and start in a couple of weeks. One person turned us down and decided to stay at his current company. I was going to offer the job to our next best candidate, but Mark (one of my superstars who helped

keep a log of ~의 일지를 기록하다(여기서 log는 일지, 일정 등을 의미) **make a deal** 합의(협상)하다 **batching** 일괄처리

interview) said the next best candidate didn't fit well with our current team. He suggested we keep looking for a more qualified candidate."

"Since you said to hire tough and never lower my standards, I asked Kim to begin the process of finding the right person for our last open position. And yes, I'm really excited about the two new team members."

"I also tried several of your time management tips. I kept a log of where I was spending my time and discovered I was spending a lot of time on things that weren't important. I also found one particular person in our office interrupted me at least six times a day. I showed her my log of how many times we were talking to each other in a day, and she couldn' t believe she called me that often."

"So, we made a deal to talk at 10 a.m. and 3 p.m. only. I guess you would call that 'batching.' "

"I also cut our weekly team meeting time in half. We normally allow an hour for our meeting, and we seem to go the full hour whether we need to or not. This week, I said we needed to cover everything faster and be finished in 30 minutes. Well, you know what? We did it. We started with our most important items and finished them all. That gave everyone on the team an extra 30 minutes that day,

cynical troops 냉소적인 부대원(여기서는 미덥지 않은 반응을 보이는 직원들)
chuckle 킬킬 웃다 **as though** ~인 것처럼 **swallow your pride** 자존심을 삼
키고, 즉 자존심을 버리고

· · ·

I do feel like I'm more in control of my time now. '나는 이제 더 잘 통제
할 수 있는 것 같다' feel이라는 농사 앞에 do라는 동사를 사용한 것은 강조하
기 위함이다.

· · ·

A head hunter just called me and offered me a great job!
That's a good deal.
방금 헤드헌터가 전화했는데 좋은 일자리를 주겠대!
그거 아주 대단하구나.

deal은 회화에서 거래라는 뜻 말고도 다양하게 사용된다.

which we used for uninterrupted planning."

"We wanted to test your theory that we could accomplish in 30 minutes of uninterrupted time what would normally take us 90 minutes to do while being interrupted. The theory worked in reality! Some of my cynical troops weren't sure that we accomplished in 30 minutes what normally took us 90, but everybody agreed that we at least doubled our productivity in those 30 minutes. That's a good deal."

"See, Tony. I was listening to you, and those were some great ideas. I do feel like I'm more in control of my time now, but I still have a way to go. I also bought a book on time management to read when I find the time."

"So now you're a comedian?" Tony chuckled. "You did make some great choices last week. It sounds as though the new people have the talent and desire to be on your team. And you made some better choices in how you spent your time. Good job!"

"Now, if I were you, I would approach Chad and Jeni about your open position. You already know they're superstars and will fit in with your team. You may have to swallow your pride when you ask them to come back, but I think it's a good idea."

let's see 글쎄요, 어디 보자 **leaf** (책의 페이지 등을)빨리 넘기다 **come on board** '승선하다' 라는 뜻으로 여기서는 '새로운 직원이 팀에 들어온다' 는 것을
의미

"Look in your spiral notebook at the notes you made when you talked to Chad and Jeni. They mentioned three things that they expected from you. What were they?"

"Well, let's see," I said, leafing back to the front of the book. "They said they needed me to hire good people, coach every member of the team to become better, and dehire the people who aren't carrying their share of the load. Is that what you were asking?" ·

"Yes," Tony said. "And how have 'we' done in those three areas?"

"I think I've made great progress in hiring other good people to be on the team," I answered. "Tony, you've taught me well and I'm now hiring tough. Kim also was a great support throughout the process, and I really feel good about the two new people who are coming on board."

"As far as coaching every team member to become better, I think I've made a little progress. I'm paying more attention to the superstars and middle stars. But I really haven't focused very much on coaching my good performers."

"Of course, I had to dehire Todd. Amazingly, I thought he was a superstar until I found out others on the team were covering for him. I guess that just proves I was

dehire 해고하다   **ensure** 확실하게 하다   **encouragingly** 힘을 북돋아주는 **reminder** 상기시키는 조언 **be/get caught up in something** 갇히다, 꼼짝 못 하다   **overlook** (결점, 실수 등을)못보고 지나가다   **regardless of** ~을 개의치 않고, 상관없이 **scorecard** 성적표, 채점표

spending too much time in management land."

"Before I begin more dehiring, I need to better define my expectations and ensure that the proper training and tools are in place. Through this entire process, I discovered that the performance reviews I've been giving don't accurately reflect performance. So, I have a lot of work to do in the dehiring area."

"Well, Jeff, it sounds as though you're at least making progress in addressing the three things Chad and Jeni suggested. Great job," my mentor said encouragingly.

"For the remainder of our time today, let's focus on how you can coach every member of the team to become better. Now, I'm not talking about performance improvement sessions. I'm talking about recognition of, and communication to, everyone on the team."

"A few weeks ago we talked about a place called 'management land' and how sometimes we get caught up in the things happening in management land while we overlook important things on the team. Here are two facts you should never forget, regardless of your title or position:

1. "Your scorecard as a leader is the result of your team.

   You are needed; you are important. But you get paid

subordinate 부하 **cumulatively** 점증적으로 **a couple of** 두서넛의

• • •

you get paid for what your subordinates do, not necessarily what you do. '네 임금에는 네가 한 일뿐만 아니라 네 부하 직원들이 한 것도 포함되어 있다' not necessarily는 '꼭 ~한 것이 아니라' 의 뜻이다.
don't get me wrong. '날 오해하지 마세요'
needs to be done is getting done '해야 할 일을 마치는 것'

for what your subordinates do, not necessarily what you do."

2. "You need your team more than your team needs you. Don't get me wrong—you need each other, but cumulatively, the 17 people on your team accomplish much more than you do."

"To make my point, answer a couple of questions. First, what percentage of the work that needs to be done is getting done while you're here with me this morning?" As always, Tony's questions went right to the heart of the issue."

"I think they're probably getting about 95 percent of the work accomplished, even while I'm not there," I admitted.

"Okay, I would agree—ninety-five percent is probably an accurate number. Some of your people may say 105 percent—they get more done while you're away—maybe so, but let' s go with your 95 percent."

"Now, let's suppose your 17 people were here with me, and you were the only one left at the office. What percentage of the work would be getting done then?" he asked."

"Not much! I would probably get about 10 percent of the work done," I responded as honestly as I could.

entrust 맡기다, 위탁하다 **portion** 일부, 부분 **analogy** 비유에 의한 설명
bucket of motivation 동기의 양동이 **overflow** 가득차다, 넘치다 **desperately** 몹시, 필사적으로 **dipper** 국자(=ladle) **cynicism** 냉소, 비꼬는 말
negativism 부정주의 **drain** 소모시키다, 고갈시키다

• • •

they have entrusted portion of their life to you. '그 사람들은 인생의 일부
분을 너에게 맡겼다'
become the very best. 최고 중의 최고가 되어라. very는 최고라는 것을 더욱
강조하기 위해 사용되었다.

"So your team is accomplishing 95 percent, and you can only accomplish 10 percent? Then who needs who the most? Obviously you need each other, but never forget that your job is to help each team member become better at the job they've chosen. They have entrusted a portion of their life to you, and it's your job to help them grow, personally and professionally. So you need to do everything you can to help them become the very best!"

"Follow me on this analogy: Every person has a bucket of motivation. That bucket can be filled to overflowing, or it can be empty and desperately need filling. Sometimes the buckets have leaks…and those buckets lose motivation as fast as you can try to motivate."

"Every person also has a dipper. In fact some people have these great big, long dippers that they enjoy putting into other people's buckets. Their dippers represent cynicism, negativism, confusion, stress, doubt, fear, anxiety, and any other thing that can drain someone's desire and motivation."

"As a leader, your job is to keep everyone's bucket filled. You are the Chief Bucket-Filler, and the best way to fill buckets is with excellent communication. In fact, there are four things you have to do if you're going to keep your

shotgun hole 총알 구멍 **inconsistency** 불일치, 모순 **appraisal** (노사 간의) 업적평가 **be sincere** 진실해라

team members' motivation buckets full."

"First, a full bucket requires knowing what are the main things that are important to doing a good job. We talked about this before, and you and your team have now identified the main things. But if people don't know what the main thing is, their motivation bucket will leak like a bucket full of shotgun holes. A leader with focus and direction fills buckets. A leader who creates confusion and inconsistency has a dipper that drains people's buckets."

"Second, to keep buckets filled, you need to provide the bucket holders with feedback on how they're doing. You may think a performance appraisal will keep a bucket full, but it won't. Performance appraisals may fill a bucket for a short period of time, but the bucket will have leaks in it after a few days. Don't get me wrong—performance reviews are important and necessary to document performance, but they don't provide long-term motivation."

"People need to know how they're doing all the time, not just at performance review time. But here's a warning: you can have great intentions to fill buckets and yet be draining buckets if you don't follow the rules of effective feedback."

"Be sincere. If you're not sincere about your feedback,

see through ~을 통하여(관통하여)보다 **scratch** 할퀴다, 긁다 **tip over** 뒤집어엎다 **aligned with** ~과 줄(선)을 맞추다

· · ·

Neither side can reach an agreement. We've been at a standstill for a week.
Don't forget this. feedback must be timely.
양쪽이 서로 동의하지 못했어. 그래서 일주일은 손 놓고 있어야 했지.
명심하게. 피드백은 정확한 시점에 해야 해.

people will see through you like a crystal glass. Insincere feedback is a great big dipper into someone's bucket."

"To fill buckets, your feedback has to be specific. If you're not specific with your praise, the bucket will not fill up. Why? Because the bucket holder will tip over the bucket while scratching his or her head, wondering what you're talking about."

"Feedback must be timely. The more time you wait to fill the bucket, the more other people's dippers will get into the bucket. Then you'll have to work twice as hard to fill it back up."

"Feedback must be aligned with the receiver's value system. Don't try to fill someone's bucket with something that's important to you but not to them. Bucket filling is in the eye of the bucket holder, not the bucket filler."

"The third thing you have to do to keep your team members' buckets filled is to let them know you care about them and the job they do. There are a gazillion ways to show you care and fill your team's buckets. Of course, the paycheck they get fills their buckets, but the buckets will dry up if you only bucket-fill on days that you hand them a paycheck. Find those bucket fillers that work best with your team, and then use them to fill their

go a long way ~에 큰 효과가 있다

. . .

A positive note of recognition goes a long way to filling a bucket. '칭찬
이 담긴 긍정적인 메모를 건네는 것은 양동이를 채우는 데 큰 효과가 있다'

buckets often."

"Here are a dozen ways to show your team members you care about them—they seem to work well for other bucket fillers I know:

Involve people in major decisions. Listen to them— they often have the best ideas anyway.

Memorize facts about the bucket holder and their family. People enjoy sharing what's happening in their families. Let them fill their own buckets while you listen.

Make coffee for your team. Making coffee is a pretty simple act that people appreciate—it's an easy bucket filler.

Send thank you notes to team members at home. People normally only get bills and junk mail at home. A positive note of recognition goes a long way to filling a bucket.

Send bucket holders a Thanksgiving card. Your

property 자산 **in honor of** ~경의를 표하며, ~를 위한 **wall of fame** 명예의
전당 **platinum** 백금(보통은 '최고' , '최상품' 이라는 표현으로 사용된다)

• • •

keep it current and well stocked. '항상 최신의 것으로 잘 채워 놔라'

• • •

One hand washes the other.

비즈니스에서 서로에게 이익이 되는 전략이나 거래를 win/win이라고 많이
표현 한다. 위의 표현은 주로 뉴욕의 비즈니스맨들이 많이 사용한다. '한 손이
다른 한 손을 씻는다', 즉 서로 없어서는 안 될 정도로 도움이 되는 관계를 의
미한다.

success is dependent on them—who else at work would you be more thankful for?

🪣 Ask your superstars—if they're interested—to become mentors for middle stars or falling stars. This is a win/win—everyone's buckets get filled.

🪣 Keep a camera close by to record significant bucket-filling events.

🪣 Plant a tree on company property in honor of your team.

🪣 Create a library of books, tapes, and magazines, and keep it current and well stocked so team members can fill their own buckets.

🪣 Create a 'wall of fame' with pictures of your team members and their families.

🪣 Follow the platinum bucket-filling rule: Treat people the way they wish to be treated.
Spend time with all your team members. Sometimes

being around 어울리다, 같이 지내다 **consistently** 시종일관

· · ·

that's the way 적극적으로 호응이나 동의를 표할 때 '그거야' 정도의 의미로 해석할 수 있다.

· · ·

I've never seen any commercials for this product. I heard about it through word-of-mouth.
That's the way it works.
난 이 상품의 광고를 본 적이 없어. 그냥 입소문으로 알게 된 거지.
바로 그게 효과가 있다는 거야.

simply being around and showing that you care about them will automatically fill their buckets.

"The fourth and final bucket-filling requirement is for the team to know how well it's doing as a team. Everyone wants to be on a winning team. Make sure team members consistently know whether the team is accomplishing its objectives or not."

"If you will fulfill the four bucket-filling requirements— know the main things, give feedback on performance, provide recognition for doing a good job, and comm-unicate the team score—your team members will be asking you what they can do to help fill your bucket. That's the way it works. The more buckets you fill, the more your bucket is filled."

Tony glanced at his watch. "Well once again, our time is up. So, what are you going to do before next week?"

"Several things. First, I'm going to call Jeni and Chad to see if they're interested in returning to the team. I'm going to share with them the changes I'm making, and will continue to make, to become a better leader."

"I really like your bucket-filling analogy. In fact, I'm going to share it with my team. If we will keep our dipp-

I may even give them a bucket and dipper to drive home the analogy and have some fun. '이 비유를 가정에서도 실천하도록 직원들에게 양동이와 국자를 사줄까 봐요. 그럼 재미있을 것 같아요'

ers out of each other's buckets, I think we can all be more motivated, productive and happy. I may even give them a bucket and dipper to drive home the analogy and have some fun," I said.

"Great, Jeff, and good luck with Jeni and Chad. I hope that works out well for you. Next week is our last session. We'll spend our time talking about you and what you can do to accomplish your personal goals. I look forward to seeing you then."

The more bucket you fill, the more your bucket is filled. '당신이 더 많은 양동이를 채울수록 당신의 양동이도 더 많이 채워질 것이다'

FILL LOTS OF BUCKETS

✓ *4 Ways to fill buckets :*
  1. Know the main things
  2. Give feedback on
    performance
  3. Provide recognition
  4. Communicate the team
    score

✓ *The more buckets you fill,*
the more your bucket is filled.

beam 빛을 발하다, 밝게 미소 짓다 **head for** ~를 향해가다 **protest** 항의하다, 이의를 제기하다 **uneasy with** 거북해하다, 어색해하다

• • •

I could tell Tony was uneasy with my praise. ‘토니가 내 칭찬에 어색해하는 것을 알 수 있었다’ I could tell…은 I knew(알았다, 알 수 있었다)의 의미로 사용한다.
boola-boola 자신이 굳이 말하지 않아도 상대방이 알 수 있는 것을 설명할 때 생략의 의미로 사용하는 표현이다.

Enter the Learning Zone

"Welcome, Jeff. It's your graduation day," beamed Tony as we shook hands and headed for his library. "The last time I went to your graduation, I told you the learning was just beginning. The same thing applies now, even after all the years of experience you have. Truth be known, I've probably learned more in our sessions than you have. Thank you for allowing me to share with you."

"Wait! Don't thank me," I protested. "You gave your time and knowledge to me!"

I could tell Tony was uneasy with my praise.

"Well, enough of the boola-boola," he said. "What happened last week at work?"

"Well, the best news is Jeni is coming back to the company. explained the changes I was making in how I lead the team. Then, I think she called several of her friends to see if I was really doing what I had outlined in

rub off on ~에 영향을 끼치다 **brainstorm** 머리를 맞대고 생각하다 **pitch** 음조

· · ·

Not only was it a fun exercise, it definitely made a point. ‘그것은 재미있 을 뿐만 아니라 확실히 효과가 있었어요’
That's about it. ‘그 정도입니다’

· · ·

My boss gave me a pay hike. Now I'll be making twice as much money! That's the good deal.
사장임이 임금을 인상해준대. 이제 돈을 두 배로 벌게 됐어!
아주 잘 됐네.

our conversation — and to find out if it was making a difference. She called on Wednesday, saying she really wanted to come back to the team. She starts in two weeks. That's a good deal."

"The new hires are doing great. They're full of enthusiasm, and it's rubbing off on the rest of the team…including me. It was worth the time and effort to hire tough and get the right people on board."

"I shared your analogy of the bucket and the dipper with the team. Then we brainstormed some of our own rules for bucket-filling and what to do when someone gets their dipper in your bucket. Not only was it a fun exercise, it definitely made a point. A couple of times last week I heard people say, 'Get your dipper out of my bucket!' when a negative or cynical comment was made."

"That's about it. Things are going pretty smoothly now that we have focus."

"That's good news, Jeff. Remember I told you this last session would be all about you?" Tony's tone was back to its serious pitch. "We've spent seven sessions talking about your team, your leadership style, and how to get results from others."

"Now let's focus on what you can do to achieve the

commend 칭찬하다 **at the end of your rope** 로프에 끝자락에 있는(아주 질 박한 상황에 있는) **out of the blue** 우울한 상태를 벗어나 **most likely** 모르면 몰라도, 십중팔구 **forceful** 힘 있는 **comfort zone** 안전지대

• • •

Ground hog day '봄이 시작되는 날' '그라운드 호그' 라는 포유동물이 있는데 이 동물이 겨울잠 후 땅위로 올라오는 날을 Ground hog day라고 부른다. 동명의 영화가 우리나라에서는 〈사랑의 블랙홀〉이라는 제목으로 소개되었다. **a forceful enemy to your potential is your comfort zone.** '자네 안에 잠재되어 있는 가장 강력한 적은 자네의 안전지대라네'

goals you have for yourself."

"First, I want to commend you. It took courage for you to call me several weeks ago. You might not have called unless you were at a point where you had nothing to lose, but you still had the courage to call. I understand that feeling of being at the end of your rope. I've been there before and made a similar call, out of the blue, to an old friend. If you hadn't had the courage to make the call, most likely nothing would have changed except you'd probably be even more frustrated. Anyway, I'm glad you called."

"Did you see the movie Ground Hog Day—the one where Bill Murray lives the same day over and over again?"

"Yes, pretty funny movie," I said.

"Well, that's the way many people live their lives," Tony explained. "They wake up and do the same things over and over and over—because that's where they're comfortable—until it's time to retire.

"Jeff, you have too much potential to be living Ground Hog Day over and over."

"A forceful enemy to your potential is your comfort zone. When you first came to my home eight weeks ago,

complacent 자기만족의, 흡족한 **learning zone** 학습지대 **made up** 완성된,
완벽한 **proof** 증거 **scarce** 드문, 진귀한, 부족한 **abundance of** 많은, 풍부한

without knowing it, you described what it was like to be in the comfort zone. And then things changed at work, and the comfort zone was no longer comfortable. You didn't know what to do or where to go."

"For you to be the very best, you cannot allow yourself to become complacent in your comfort zone. You need to be reaching for improvement. To fulfill your potential, you need to move out of your comfort zone and into 'the learning zone.' "

"Let me explain. There are three rooms in the learning zone. The first room is the reading room. Look around this library—there are more than a thousand books in here. More than half of those books are about management and leadership. Executives call me to help them solve business problems. I've never 'made up' a solution. None of their problems are unique. The value I offer is the wisdom of all the people who have written these books."

"You learn more by reading more. I'm living proof that the more you learn, the more you earn.

"Did you know most people don't read one non-fiction book in a year? Not one. You'd think books must be scarce or expensive. But there is an abundance of books at every public library, waiting for people to simply walk in and

no-brainer (속어로)쉬운 일, 간단한 일 **assume** (역할, 임무 등을)맡다 **discipline** 훈련 **principal** 원칙

• • •

**The question is do you have the discipline to set aside time every day
to read.** '문제는 당신이 매일 독서를 위한 시간을 마련하는 훈련을 하는가
입니다'

check them out—at no charge—free!"

"Now let's suppose you decided to read one book a month on management or leadership. Most books are between 12 and 20 chapters, so you'd be reading about half a chapter a day, which would take you about 10 minutes. During the next year, you'd have read 12 books. Do you think you'd know more about management and leadership if you read 12 books a year on the subject?"

This was a rare no-brainer question for our Monday mornings. "Of course," I said.

"When the next job opening at a higher position in the company comes up, would you be better prepared to assume that role?"

"Of course!"

"See, Jeff, the question is NOT do you have the time or money. The question is do you have the DISCIPLINE to set aside time every day to read. In your case, you probably won't retire for at least 15 years. In 15 years, you could read 180 books just by reading half a chapter a day. Make it a priority to read, and your knowledge will likely make you the obvious choice for the next promotion."

"The second room in the learning zone is the listening room. Did you know that the principle reasons executives

arrogance 거만, 불손 **out of control egos** 자기 통제불능 **insensitivity** 무
감각, 둔함 **trap** 덫 **hearse** 영구차 **rack** 선반 **legacy** 유산

• • •

it's just a thought. '그냥 내 생각엔 그래' 충고나 조언, 혹은 자기 의사를 상
대방에게 가볍게 던질 때 사용하는 표현이다.
There are reasons why hearses don't have luggage racks! '영구차에 선
반이 없는데는 이유가 있는 거예요' 뒷문장과 연결해 생각해보면 자신의 유산
은 죽을 때 가져가는 것이 아니라는 것을 설명하고 있다.

• • •

I hear Rob can be a real shark.
I know. but I don't allow myself to fall into his trap.
롭이 정직한 친구가 아니라는 소리가 있어.
나도 알아. 하지만 절대 그 친구 속임수에 빠지진 않을 거야.

shark는 정직하지 못한 비즈니스맨을 뜻하는 단어로 사용되기도 한다.

fail are arrogance, out-of-control egos, and insensitivity?"

"They forget to take the time to listen to their people. Soon they become insensitive to the needs and desires of the individuals on the team. Arrogance, out-of-control egos, and insensitivity are part of the management land trap. Don't allow yourself to fall into that trap — listen to your people!"

"A few other comments about listening. First, you tend to listen better when you attend outside seminars and conferences. Any time you gather new information, you can make better decisions."

"Second, you can also learn to listen better by making better use of your time while you're in your car. The average person spends over 500 hours per year in their car. That's a lot of time. Maybe if you spent some of that time listening to a motivational or inspirational audiotape, it would have a greater influence on you than listening to talk radio or music. It's just a thought..."

"The third room in the learning zone is the giving room. I strongly feel you cannot succeed without giving back," Tony continued. "There are reasons why hearses don't have luggage racks! Your legacy will be what you leave others. When we started these sessions, one of the

accountable 책임감 있는 **measurable** 측정 가능한 **obtainable** 얻을 수 있는, 획득할 수 있는 **rhetorically** 웅변조로

requirements was that you would have to teach others what I was teaching you. My purpose in making that a requirement was so you would become more accountable. The more you teach, the more accountable you become to what you're teaching. Teaching is good for you!"

"I realize it's easy to agree we need to become life-long learners. But the facts are that nothing is going to change unless you set specific goals for improvement."

"You may have heard the story of people who went to the airport to wait for their ship to come in. The only problem is, ships don't go to airports! If you want your ship to come in, you've got to go where the ships are. In personal improvement, the ships are in goals—specific, measurable, and obtainable goals."

"I've found that goals can become the strongest force for self-motivation—they are your track to run your course. Yet less than five percent of all people set specific goals, and fewer than five percent will write their goals down on paper."

"If goals are so important, why don't more people set them?" Tony asked, rhetorically. "I think there are four main reasons why people fail to set goals. First, people fail to set goals because they don't know the importance of

prelude 전조, 준비행위, 서곡 **be a prelude to something** ~의 전조이다

· · ·

don't take this to an extreme. '너무 극단적으로 받아들이진 마라' don't take…는 '~하게 받아들이지 마라' 의 의미로 자주 사용한다. ex)don't take this so seriously. '너무 심각하게 받아들이지 마라'

· · ·

We finally caved and gave them everything they want.
Cheer up! Failure is a prelude to success.
결국 그들이 원하는 대로 다 내주고 말았어요.
기운 내. 실패는 성공의 어머니잖아.

goal setting. Every great accomplishment I know about has begun with a goal written down on a sheet of paper. Achieving the goal is automatic. Setting the goal is the issue."

"Second, most people don't know how to set goals. After each session, I asked you to write down what actions you were going to take the next week. I did that because writing clarifies the goal and commits you to it."

"Third, sometimes people don't set goals because they're afraid of failure. If you have no goals, you're not risking failure. I think we should do the opposite—fail faster and more often. Failure is a prelude to success. To become more successful, we have to fail more often…but don't take this to an extreme. I'm talking about setting goals that will help us become more successful even if we fail to accomplish the goal."

"Fourth, goals require people to leave their comfort zone. That can be scary for many people because it often involves having to learn new skills."

"Nothing would please me more than to watch you become a fantastic goal setter and goal achiever. You can become a leader who has balance in your life. You can become a great role model for others to follow. But over

fairway 골프장의 잔디밭 **divot** (골프 클럽에 맞아)뜯긴 잔디 조각, 패인 곳
gust 한바탕 부는 바람, 돌풍 **bunker** 골프장의 코스 중 모래가 있는 우묵한
곳 **putt** (골프)공을 가볍게 치는 것

· · ·

Pollyanna 미국 여류작가 엘리노 포터의 동명 소설 《Pollyanna》의 여주인공
으로 극단적인 낙천주의자의 대명사로 불린다.

the years, I've learned that most people don't want to follow someone who loses their health or their family because they work all the time. People want to follow people who are balanced in all areas, not just work."

"My final thought for you is this: Stay positive! Of course you will become discouraged again somewhere along the way. Just don't give up."

"The world is not for Pollyannas. Bad things happen to even the best people. You know how much I enjoy golf. Well, I think golf is a great teacher of life's lessons as well as leadership lessons. And, I've learned that in every round of golf, three bad things are going to happen that are not deserved."

"You may hit the ball in the middle of the fairway only to discover the ball in an old divot. Or, you hit the perfect shot right before the wind gusts, and your shot lands just short, buried in the bunker. Or perhaps your perfect putt moves off course because someone didn't take time to fix their ball mark."

"Similar unfair things happen in business. The question is not, 'Are unfair things going to happen?' The question is, 'How are you going to react to whatever happens?' "

"I have one last story for you:"

Ph.D 박사학위 **nugget** (천연 귀금속의)덩어리, 귀한 부분 **perimeter** 주변, 경
계선

. . .

realizing that they really didn't have it bad after all. '결국 그들이 정말
로 나쁜 것을 가진 것이 아니라는 사실을 깨달으면서'

"I once knew an older woman who I would consider one of the wisest and most positive persons I've ever known. She didn' t have much money or formal education, nor did she work outside the home. Yet she had earned a Ph.D in common sense and wisdom."

"One of the nuggets of wisdom from this old friend that I will always remember is how to face problems and be positive, no matter the situation."

"She loved to tell the story of how everyone could go to a field—about the size of a football field—and line up around the perimeter. While standing on the edge of the field, each person is given the opportunity to throw their problems into the middle of the field. Once all the problems have been thrown in, you have your choice of which ones to pick up and take home. Most people will probably pick up their own problems and go back home, realizing that they really didn' t have it that bad after all."

"You know, I think she's right on the money with her story! So much of life is about attitude and how we handle what life throws our way. Life is good—even when a situation appears to be the worst. Stay positive and help make another's life better!"

"So, Jeff, we are about out of time. And, for the last

suspect 짐작하다   **commitment** 헌신, 약속   **brass bucket** 황동 양동이
engrave (금속, 돌 등에 문자도안을) 새기다, 장식하다   **at the risk of** ~을 무릅
쓰고, ~을 희생하고   **corny** 진부한, 촌스러운

• • •

role model 미국기업의 경우 신입사원의 우선 과제는 회사 내에서 role mo-
del을 찾아 그를 따르는 것이다. 이것이 성공의 지름길이라고 믿는다.

214

time, I'll ask my question: What are you going to do differently?"

"Well, Tony, I think you saved your best story for last, and I think your friend is probably right."

I suspected you would ask me what I would do differently one more time, so I came prepared. I've reviewed my notes from all the previous sessions, and here are my commitments:"

"And after this week's session, I'm going to add two more:

 ✓ I live in the learning zone.

 ✓ I am a positive role model for others."

"Wonderful, Jeff! My, you have come a long way in the past eight weeks," Tony said, standing and shaking my hand.

"Before I leave, I have something for you in my car," I said. "I'll be right back."

"Here, Tony. This is for you," I said, handing him a gift-wrapped box.

Tony opened the present—a big brass bucket with Tony's initials engraved on the front. It was filled to overflowing with 30 or so small gifts.

"At the risk of sounding corny, this gift represents what

a lump beginning in my throat. '목이 메다'

So long! 안녕(good-bye), 친한 사이에서 쓰는 표현으로 보통 어려운 사람(윗사람)에게는 잘 쓰지 않는다.

you have done for me the past eight weeks," I explained, a lump beginning in my throat. "You filled my bucket with your gifts of insight and wisdom."

"So my question to you is, 'When can we meet again?' "

"Well, remember—when we began our sessions you committed to teach others what I would be teaching you. Do that and then we'll get together. Thank you for the bucket and gifts, Jeff. I am honored that you called me and allowed me to work with you."

I took a deep breath as I walked outside and turned to wave. "So long, Tony. See you soon!"

Jeff Leadership Commitments

✓ I am responsible for my actions and my team's performance, no matter what the circumstances.

✓ I keep the main thing the main thing.

✓ I have a positive relationship with my boss.

✓ I escape from management land and stay in tune with my people.

✓ I recognize and reward superstar activity.

✓ I address problems in a pro-active manner.

✓ I do what's right even when no one is watching.

✓ I realize that everything I do counts toward my leadership score.

✓ I hire tough.

✓ I am an excellent time manager.

✓ I fill other's buckets.

LIVE IN THE LEARNING ZONE

✓ Get out of the comfort zone

✓ Read 10 minutes a day

✓ Listen to people

✓ Give back

✓ Set goals

✓ Stay positive

serve as ~의 역할을 하다 turning point 전환기 take over 인계받다
luxury 사치 set up ~을 세우다, 정하다

Epilogue

Present day...

My eight Monday Mornings with Tony served as the turning point in my career. His gentle wisdom has guided my actions and my path during the past two years.

Six months ago, I was promoted and Jeni, who left our company and then came back, took over my old position.

Most people don't have—and will never have—the luxury of a mentor like Tony. My desire is that you will be able to learn from him and pass on this knowledge to others.

Now I can make my call to Tony to set up our next meeting...

Wisdom from Tony
A Collection of Quotations

"When it comes to leading people,
there is no problem that is unique to you."
Page 37

"Even though your responsibilities increase
when you become a manager, you lose some of the rights
or freedoms you may have enjoyed in the past."
Page 43

"A real leader spends his time fixing the problem
instead of finding who to blame."
Page 45

"When you write things down,
you commit to doing them. If you simply
tell me what you want to do, there is

really no commitment to getting it done."
Page 47

"When you depend on another's perceptions
to match your expectations, you're setting yourself
up for disappointment."
Page 61

"People quit people before they quit companies."
Page 61

"Take the time to manage your boss
the same way you manage your subordinates."
Page 65

"One of the 'main things' for a leader is to eliminate
confusion."
Page 81

"You have to escape from management land and get in
touch with your people."
Page 83

"Your job is not to lower the bottom
by adjusting for and accommodating
the lowest performing employees. You should be
raising the tip by recognizing and rewarding
superstar behaviors!"
Page 89

"Doing the right thing isn't always easy in fact
sometimes it's real hard but just remember that
doing the right thing is always right."
Page 107

"Everything you do matters because your team is
watching… and depending on you to do the right thing."
Page 113

"Guard your integrity as if it's your most precious
leadership possession, because that is what it is."
Page 115

"The most important thing you do as a leader is
to hire the right people."
Page 131

"Never lower your standards just to fill a position.

You will pay for it later."

Page 137

"One of the major sources of stress, anxiety,

and unhappiness comes from feeling like

your life is out of control."

Page 145

"If you want to make better use of your time,

you need to be looking for the small increments of

time…a minute here, five minutes there, etc."

Page 145

"You are the Chief Bucket-Filler,

and the best way to fill buckets is with excellent

communication."

Page 179

"For you to be the very best, you cannot allow

yourself to become complacent in your comfort zone.

You need to be reaching for improvement."

Page 201

"So much of life is about attitude and how we handle
what life throws our way. Life is good even when a
situation appears to be the worst."

Page 213

The CornerStone Principles of Leadership

Values Principles

The Principle of Integrity—Results improve in proportion to the level of trust earned by the leader.

The Principle of Responsibility—Results improve when leaders and their followers are held accountable for their actions.

The Principle of Commitment—Results improve to the extent that the leader hires and develops talented people.

The Principle of Vision—Results improve when leaders establish a crystal—clear vision with a convincing reason to embrace the vision.

Synergy Principles

The Principle of Communication—Results improve when followers understand their role and are rewarded for their accomplishments.

The Principle of Conflict Resolution — Results improve when the leader removes obstacles inhibiting followers.

The Principle of Optimism — Results improve in proportion to the self-esteem and attitude of the leader.

The Principle of Change Management — Results improve to the extent the leader embraces change and makes change positive.

Investment Principles

The Principle of Empowerment — Results improve as followers are allowed to accept responsibility for their actions.

The Principle of Courage — Results improve in proportion to the leader' s ability to confront issues affecting his followers.

The Principle of Example — Results improve when the leader is a positive role model.

The Principle of Preparation — Results improve to the extent that leaders develop themselves and their followers.

Keynotes & Seminars with David Cottrell

David Cottrell is a thought provoking and electrifying professional speaker. His powerful wisdom and insights on leadership and customer service have made him a highly sought after keynote speaker and seminar leader.

David Cottrell's seminars are customized to reinforce your company mission, vision, and values. The content is practical for team leaders, managers, supervisors and sales professionals.

˙acknowledgement 감사의 글 mold ~을 본뜨다 grateful 감사하는
expertise 전문가

Acknowledgements

Over the years, I have been blessed with some wonderful mentors. My success has been molded and formed by those who always seem to have the time to listen and the wisdom to share. I thank the following people for being my mentors:

Alice Adams, Paul Damoc, Ty Deleon, Louis Kruger, Mark Layton, Joe Miles, Wallace Moorehand, Tony Van Roekel, and Tod Taylor.

I am also grateful to the people whose expertise made Monday Morning Leadership a reality: Alice Adams and Juli Baldwin—my editors. Defae Weaver—book designer, Keith Crabtree—cover designer and Barbara Bartlett—my assistant who held everything together while this book was being completed.

To all of you whom I have named, please accept my deepest thanks.

To each person who reads this book, best wishes as you become a positive role model, mentor, and friend for the people around you.

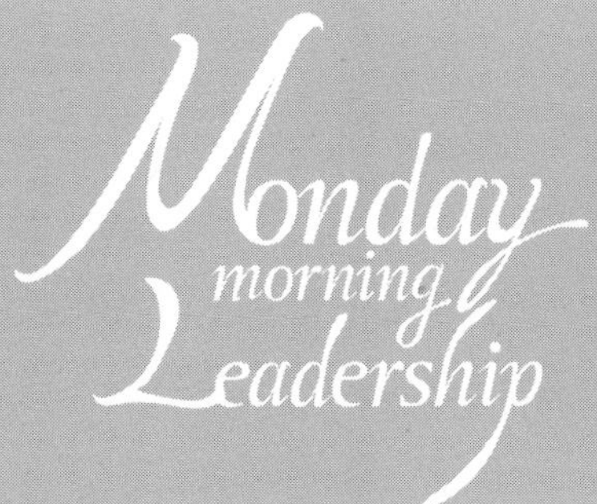

먼데이 모닝 리더십 : 8일간의 기적
〈한글 요약문〉

프롤로그

나(Jeff)는 포춘 지가 선정한 500대 기업 안에 드는 회사에 들어가 성공한 관리자가 되기까지 열심히 일했다. 그러나 곧 슬럼프에 빠지게 됐고, 그것은 팀에도 영향을 끼치게 되었다. 일은 느리게 진행되었고, 실적에 대한 압박감으로 팀원 모두가 참을 수 없는 지경에 이르렀다.

나는 스스로의 리더십에 대해 강한 회의가 들었고, 나를 도와줄 사람이 절실히 필요했다. 그러던 어느 토요일, 나는 골프장에서 아버지의 친구이자 성공한 비즈니스 리더인 토니를 보게 되었다. 은퇴 전 토니는 '부실기업 회생 전문가'로 일했으며, 지금은 최고경영자들을 코칭하는 일을 하고 있었다. 전문 분야에서의 성공으로 토니는 백만장자가 되었을 뿐 아니라 다른 사람들을 많이 도와주었기 때문에 지역사회의 존경을 받고 있었다.

토니는 내가 꼭 닮고 싶은 이상형이었다. 나 역시 그처럼 사람들에게 존경받는 대화 상대이자 멘토가 되고 싶었던 것이다. 예전에 내 대학 졸업식 날 보낸 토니의 축하 카드에는 의논 상대가 필요하면 언제든지 연락하라는 내용이 적혀 있었다.

나는 망설인 끝에 토니에게 전화를 했고, 토니는 흔쾌히 의논 상대가 돼주기로 했다. 대신 그는 조건을 두 가지 달았다. 8주

동안 매주 월요일 아침마다 토니의 집에 올 것과 토니와의 대화에서 얻은 교훈과 경험을 다른 사람에게 나누라는 것이었다.

1. 운전사와 승객

토니와의 첫 만남을 위한 날, 나는 그와의 만남이 정말로 많은 일들을 변화시킬 수 있을지에 대해 회의적이었다. 나는 약속 시간인 8시 30분보다 10분 늦게 토니의 집에 도착했다. 토니는 8주 동안 수업을 하게 될 서재로 나를 안내했다. 몇 마디 말이 오고 간 후 곧 토니는 수업의 기본 규칙에 대해 말했다. 수업 시작시간과 종료시간을 꼭 지킬 것. 진실만을 말할 것. 지금까지와는 다른 방식을 시도할 것.

나는 규칙을 지킬 것을 약속하자 토니는 현재 내가 겪고 있는 어려움에 대해 듣고 싶어 했다. 그로부터 1시간에 걸쳐 나는 나에 대한 이야기를 했다. 사회에 첫발을 내디딘 후 몇 년 동안 나는 쉽게 성공했다. 에너지가 넘쳤으며 미래에 대해서도 아주 낙관적이었다. 남들보다 승진도 빨라서 관리자가 되기까지 했다.

그러나 몇 년 후 사업이 난항에 부딪히기 시작했다. 팀 구성원에는 변화가 없었지만 그 때까지 내가 무시해왔던 업무수행상의 문제들이 업무 실적에 영향을 미치기 시작했다. 나는 열심히 일

했지만 실적은 떨어지기만 했고, 팀원들과 나는 초조하고 의기
소침해졌다.

토니는 내 말을 듣고 말했다. 우선 모든 리더가 나와 같은 문
제를 가지고 있으므로 자책하는 데 시간을 낭비하지 말라는 것
과 변화하기에 전혀 늦지 않았다는 것이었다. 그리고 그는 운전
사와 승객에 대한 이야기를 했다. 승객은 자유롭게 어떤 일도 할
수 있지만 운전사는 그래서는 안 되듯이 리더 역시 마찬가지라
는 것이었다. 리더는 자신이 직면하고 있는 문제의 책임소재를
찾는 데 시간을 허비하는 사람이 아니라 그 문제를 해결하는 사
람이라는 기억하라는 것이었다.

토니는 서로가 나눈 대화를 적을 수 있도록 나에게 '토니와
함께한 월요일 아침'이라는 제목이 적힌 파란색 노트를 한 권
주었다. 토니의 집을 나섰을 때 나는 훨씬 난감한 기분이 들었
다. 우리 팀에서 일어난 모든 일들을 내 책임으로 받아들이는 일
이 너무 힘들어 보였기 때문이다. 하지만 나는 토니와 지금까지
와 다른 식으로 시도해볼 것을 약속했다.

2. 핵심과업을 상기하라

두 번째 만남에서 나는 토니에게 토니의 가르침대로 하는 것이

어렵다는 이야기를 했다. 팀에서 일어나는 모든 일들에 대한 책임이 나에게 있다는 사실을 인정하려 했지만 너무 많은 일들이 벌어져 쉽지 않았다. 우리 팀에는 직원이 15명이 있는데 2명이 결원 상태이고, 나머지 직원들이 그에 대한 일을 분담하고 있었다. 각 직원들은 열심히 일하고 있지만 실적은 오르지 않았다.

토니는 내개 몇 가지 기본적인 질문을 던졌다. 왜 2명을 결원 상태로 두며, 이전 직원들은 왜 그만두었는지 그리고 나의 우선순위는 무엇인지 말이다. 그러고 나서 토니는 자신의 경험을 이야기하며, 핵심과업이 무엇인지 계속해서 상기할 때 직원들이 효율적으로 일할 수 있다고 했다. 토니는 나에게, 직원들이 핵심과업을 무엇이라고 생각하는지 물어볼 것과 직원들이 회사를 그만두는 이유를 알아오라고 했다. 특히 직원들이 회사를 그만두는 가장 큰 이유는 바로 상사라는 사실을 알려주며, 나와 나의 상사 카렌과의 관계를 제대로 확립하는 것이 우선이라고 했다.

3. 관리자세상에서 벗어나라

세 번째 월요일 아침 나는 토니를 찾았다. 토니가 내준 과제 덕에 지난주에는 일이 어느 정도 진척이 있었다는 사실을 토니에게 말했다. 첫 번째로 나는 지난 두 달 사이에 그만둔 제니와 채드가 회사에서 일어나는 일들에 대해 불만을 가지고 있었다는 사실을 알게 됐다. 나는 그 둘을 직접 만나 이야기를 나누었는데 문제가 상사인 나였다는 것을 알고 놀랐다. 그들은 내가 유능한 직원들에게 더 많은 일을 시키면서도 적절한 피드백을 주지 않았다고 이야기했다. 또한 직원들의 업무수행상 문제점을 그냥 넘어갔던 일이 다른 직원들에게 영향을 끼쳤다고 했다.

직원관리에 대한 나의 문제점을 알게 되자 참담한 기분이 들었지만 앞으로 이러한 문제를 해결할 수 있다는 생각에 안심이 되었다. 한편 나는 지난주 수요일에 직원회의를 소집해서 직원들에게 '우리 부서의 핵심과업은?' 이라는 종이를 주고 빈칸을 채우라고 했다. 모두들 답을 썼지만 일치하는 것은 없었다. 결국 나에게는 우리 팀의 핵심과업을 규정하고 팀원들이 그것을 이해하도록 만드는 과제가 생겼다. 이 일로 나는 내 상사 카렌과 면담을 신청했다. 우리 둘은 우선 서로와의 관계를 개선하는 일부터 시작하기로 했다.

토니는 나의 이야기를 듣고 내가 잘하고 있다며 칭찬해주었다. 토니는 대다수의 관리자들이 빠지기 쉬운 함정을 '관리자세상' 이라 불렀는데, 그는 리더가 '관리자세상' 에 빠지게 되면 직원들 사이에서 일어나는 일을 분명히 알아내기 어렵다고 했다. 그 점에서 직원들과 직접 이야기를 하는 것이 얼마나 중요한지 그는 거듭 강조했다.

이어서 직원 관리에 대한 실질적인 조언이 따라왔다. 팀에는 슈퍼스타*super star*, 미들스타*middle star*, 폴링스타*falling star*라는 세 가지 유형의 직원들이 있다는 것이었다. 슈퍼스타는 보통 팀에 약 30%를 차지하는데 이들은 경험과 지식이 뛰어나고 자기 분야에서 최고가 되고자 하는 사람이다. 만약 이들에게 계속 과도한 업무를 맡기게 되면 그들이 견디지 못한다는 것이었다. 그런데 실제 많은 관리자들이 팀의 20%를 차지하는 폴링스타의 업무수준을 용인하면서 오히려 그들의 업무를 줄여주고 있다고 했다.

결론적으로 리더는 업무수행 능력이 가장 낮은 직원들의 업무량을 조절함으로써 전체적인 업무수준을 낮추는 것이 아니라 슈퍼스타의 행동이 무엇인지를 찾아내 상을 줌으로써 최고수준을 높여야 하는 것이다. 토니는 나에게 다음 과제를 내주었다. 노트에 직원들의 명단을 적고 슈퍼스타, 미들스타, 폴링스타로 분류한 뒤 가장 최근의 직원업무수행 평가서의 평가점수를 명단 옆에 기록하라는 것이었다. 그리고 지난 6개월 동안 직원들의 수상 내역이나 업무수행 향상에 관한 기록도 적으라고 했다.

4. '옳은 일을 하라' 원칙

네 번째 월요일 아침 나는 8시가 되기 전에 토니 집에 도착했다. 그 이유는 토니와의 면담시간이 더 필요하다는 생각 때문이었다. 지난주 내내 나는 거대한 수렁에 빠진 듯한 느낌이었다. 나는 토니가 이야기해준 대로 직원들을 세 분류로 나누고 업무수행 평가를 확인했는데, 이를 통해 나의 직원 평가 방법에 일관성이 없다는 사실을 알게 되었다. 그동안 직원들에 대해서 잘 알고 있다고 생각했는데 실제로는 그렇지 않았던 것이다.

수상내역과 업무수행 기록만 갖고 본다면 팀원들은 모두 미들스타에 해당하는 수준이었고, 슈퍼스타는 단 한 명뿐이었다. 그런데 이 유일한 슈퍼스타인 토드라는 직원이 문제였다. 3주 전 나는 토드가 근무 중에 술을 먹어왔다는 사실을 알게 됐고, 한번만 더 술을 먹고 근무를 하게 되면 회사를 그만둬야 한다고 그에게 경고했다.

그런데 지난 금요일 그가 또 술을 마시고 있는 것을 보게 된 것이다. 하지만 나는 그 사실을 모른 체했다. 만약 토드를 해고한다면 결원이 세 자리로 늘어나는데다 또 한 명의 슈퍼스타를 잃게 되기 때문이었다. 나는 회사 방침대로 그를 해고해야 한다는 사실을 알고 있었지만 현실적인 문제와 동정심 때문에 갈등

하고 있었다.

토니는 나의 고민에 대해 이렇게 말했다. 리더는 단기간의 편안함이 아닌 장기적이고 지속적인 성공을 위해 팀의 최고수준을 올려야 할 뿐 아니라 명확한 행동강령과 정확한 피드백이 필요하다.

더구나 토드의 일을 나만이 알고 있다는 생각은 잘못된 것이라고 토니는 말했다. 보통 팀의 문제는 맨 마지막에 가서야 관리자가 알게 되기 때문이다. 토니는 다른 팀원들이 나의 결정을 주시하고 있으며, 내가 잘못된 결정을 내리면 나는 리더로서의 도덕성을 상실하게 돼 팀원들의 신뢰를 얻거나 유지하기 힘들다고 말했다.

나는 토니의 메시지를 분명히 알아듣긴 했지만 그러한 결정을 내린다는 것이 힘들었다. 그러나 결국 인사과에 가서 이 일에 대해 논의하기로 결심하고 토니에게 직원채용에 대한 상담을 다음 주에 받을 수 있도록 부탁했다.

5. 직원채용을 까다롭게 해라

토니와의 다섯 번째 만남에서 나는 지난주에 있었던 일을 이야기했다. 지난주 토니와의 만남에서 어려운 결심을 하고 나는 인사과 직원인 킴을 만나 토드의 문제에 대해 이야기했다. 킴도 토니와 같은 의견이어서 나는 토드를 해고시키기로 결정하고, 토드와의 최종 면담시간에 동석해줄 것을 킴에게 요청했다.

토드는 '사소한 문제'로 해고하겠다는 것에 심하게 반발했고 나를 비난했지만 나와 킴은 그를 만나기 전에 이러한 상황에 대해 예상했기 때문에 절차를 무사히 수행할 수 있었다. 막상 토드를 해고하고 보니 놀라운 사실이 드러났다. 이미 미들스타 두 명이 토드의 음주 사실에 대해 알고 있었던 것이다. 결국 팀원들은 날 지켜보고 있었고 나의 도덕성이 도전을 받고 있었던 것이었다. 인사과의 킴은 우리 팀 세 명의 충원을 위해 20명의 후보를 추렸고, 채용면접을 잡았다. 주말 전까지 세 사람을 뽑을 수 있기를 기대하며 나는 오늘 토니에게 직원채용에 관한 이야기를 들으러 왔던 것이다.

토니는 지난주 나의 행동에 대해 칭찬을 했다. 그리고 직원채용과 관련한 이야기를 시작했다. 그는 회사에서 가장 큰 손실은 부적합한 직원이라고 하며, 주말까지 세 사람을 채용하고 싶다는 내 생각에 반대했다. 그는 까다롭게 직원을 채용해서 적합한 직원이 들어오도록 서두르지 말고 일을 진행하라고 말했다.

토니는 직원채용에는 333법칙이라는 게 있다고 했다. 그것은 한 직무에 최소한 3명까지 후보를 선발하고, 면접관 3명이 3번에 걸쳐 면접을 하는 것을 의미했다. 토니는 또한 각각의 면접을 아침, 점심, 저녁 등으로 시간대를 달리 잡으면 면접자들의 하루의 면모를 살펴볼 수 있을 것이라는 팁도 주었다.

그리고 면접을 볼 때 슈퍼스타를 참여시켜 그의 의견을 들어보라는 것과 적임자인지 고민이 되는 사람은 탈락시키고 다시 적합한 사람을 찾으라는 조언도 했다. 충원에만 급급해 기준을 낮추면 나중에 그 대가를 치르게 되기 때문이었다. 나는 토니의 말대로 직원채용을 하기로 결정하고 다음주에 일이 어떻게 진행됐는지 보고하기로 했다.

6. 일을 덜하거나 빨리하라

이번엔 그 어느 때보다 토니와의 월요일 만남이 무척이나 기다려졌다. 나는 토니를 만나 지난주에 있었던 일을 이야기했다. 토니의 조언대로 일을 수행했으며, 직원채용에 심혈을 기울였다는 사실을 말이다. 하지만 한 가지 이 일에 내가 너무 시간을 빼앗겼고, 다른 업무를 거의 하지 못한 사실에 대해 토니에게 도움을 요청했다.

토니는 자신의 시간은 자신이 책임을 져야 한다며 단호하게 말했다. 시간관리를 위해서는 낭비하고 있는 시간을 조금씩 찾아내라고 이야기했다. 토니는 나에게 지난 2주 동안 시간을 사용한 방식을 추적해보라고 했다.

그리고 토니는 우선순위와 정리에 관한 이야기를 시작했다. 가장 중요한 시간관리 요령 중 하나는 매일 방해받지 않고 계획할 수 있는 시간을 확보해 놓으라는 것이었다. 또한 책상 위 서류는 보관하지 말고 그 때 그 때 처리할 것, 이메일을 특정시간에 확인할 것, 일을 일괄해서 처리할 것 등을 이야기했다. 점심시간을 다른 사람들보나 1시간 전이나 후에 갖는 것도 시간을 확보할 수 있는 좋은 방법이라고 덧붙여 말했다.

그 다음 토니는 일에 몰입하는 것을 방해하는 요소들을 어떻게 제거할 것인지 이야기했다. 사무실에 사람이 찾아온다면 일어나서 선 채로 일을 처리하거나 바깥 풍경이 보이지 않게 책상을 배치하는 것, 직원이나 상관과의 면담일정표를 짜서 일을 일괄 처리하는 것이 도움이 된다는 것이었다.

또한 잦은 회의의 문제점에 대해 지적하며 그는 몇 가지 조언을 했다. 회의를 시작하면 가장 중요한 의제부터 처리할 것과 지각한 직원에게 처리한 내용을 요약해서 알려주지 말라는 것이었다. 중요한 의제를 먼저 회의하면 중요 사항을 시간에 쫓겨 처리하지 않아도 되고, 지각한 직원들을 용인하면 회의에 참석한 다른 직원들의 시간을 빼앗기 때문이다.

토니는 이 밖에도 시간을 내서 관련된 책을 읽으라고 권했다. 나는 토니의 말대로 이번 주에는 내 시간을 방해하는 요소들과 개선점에 대해서 생각해볼 것을 약속하고, 채용과정도 마무리 짓겠다고 말했다.

7. 양동이와 국자

나는 8시 30분에 정확히 토니의 집에 도착해 지난주에 있었던 일을 말하기 시작했다. 킴과 나는 지난주 채용면접을 마무리 짓고 세 후보에게 자리를 배정했다. 그 중 두 명은 2주 내로 출근하기로 했지만 한 사람은 입사를 거절했다. 나는 그 다음으로 점수가 좋은 후보에게 입사를 제의하려 했으나 우리 팀의 슈퍼스타의 의견에 따라 시간이 걸리더라도 좀더 자격을 갖춘 후보를 찾기로 결정했다.

또한 나는 지난주 내가 어디에 시간을 빼앗기고 있는지 알아낸 이야기를 했다. 나는 나를 가장 많이 방해하는 직원과 시간을 정해놓고 만나기로 했고, 매주 있었던 직원회의 시간을 반으로 줄였다. 그리고 일괄처리의 기술을 사용하자 평소 90분 걸리던 일을 30분 안에 해결할 수 있다는 사실도 알게 되었다.

토니는 지난주 나의 행동들을 칭찬하며 조언을 덧붙였다. 직원채용 과정에서 남은 한 자리에 회사를 그만두었던 슈퍼스타인 채드와 제니 중 한 명을 채용하는 것이 어떻겠냐는 것이었다. 그러고 나서 토니는 팀원에 대한 리더의 코칭 방법, 즉 커뮤니케이션에 대해 이야기하기 시작했다.

토니는, 리더란 팀원들의 동기를 채워주는 사람임을 강조했다. 그는 비유를 하나 들었다. 사람들은 각자 '동기'라는 양동이를 가지고 있는 어떤 양동이는 '동기'가 흘러넘칠 수도 있고 어떤 양동이는 텅 비어 있다는 것이다. 또한 사람들은 국자를 가지고 다른 사람의 양동이에 집어넣기를 즐기는데, 이것은 다른 사람에게 냉소, 부정적인 생각, 근심 등을 집어넣어 동기를 마르게 하는 것이라고 했다.

리더로서의 직무는 커뮤니케이션을 통해 직원들의 양동이를 채워놓는 것이라고 토니는 말했다. 양동이를 채우기 전에 리더는 우선 직원들의 양동이가 온전한 것인지, 즉 각 직원들이 자신의 핵심과업이 무엇인지 제대로 알고 있는지를 확인해야 한다고 했다. 그 다음으로는 양동이 주인에게 그것을 채우는 방법을 제시해 주어야 하는데, 리더의 업무수행 평가만으로는 양동이를 지속적으로 채울 수는 없기 때문이다. 직원들은 업무수행 평가 뿐만 아니라 평상시에도 자신이 어떻게 일하고 있는지 피드백을 받아야 하며, 리더는 올바르고 구체적인 피드백을 주어야 한다는 것이었다.

또한 피드백은 적절한 타이밍에 받는 사람의 눈높이에 맞는 것이어야만 효과적일 수 있다고 토니는 말했다. 그 다음 토니는 직원들의 양동이를 채워주기 위해서 리더가 직원들에게 관심을 가지고 있음을 보여줄 필요가 있다며, 이를 위한 12가지 방법을 이야기했다. 마지막으로 토니는 팀 성적을 팀원들에게 지속적으로 알려주는 것도 도움이 된다고 이야기했다.

나는 다음 주까지 제니와 채드의 채용에 관한 문제해결과 좀 더 나은 리더가 되기 위해 시도할 것을 토니에게 약속했다. 한편 토니는 리더가 개인적인 목표를 이루기 위해 할 수 있는 일에 대해 다음 주에 이야기하겠다며 수업시간을 끝냈다.

8. 학습지대에 머물러라

아쉽게도 토니와의 마지막 수업시간이 찾아왔다. 나는 토니에게 제니를 다시 채용하게 됐다는 사실부터 이야기했다. 그리고 새로 뽑은 직원들도 열심히 일하고 있고, 나머지 직원들까지 영향을 받아 열심히 한다는 소식을 전했다. 또한 나는 팀원들과 양동이와 국자에 대한 이야기를 나누었고, 팀원들이 그것을 긍정적으로 받아들이고 있음을 이야기했다.

내 말을 들은 후 토니는 이제 마지막 수업시간의 주제인 개인의 목표 달성에 대한 이야기를 시작했다. 최고가 되려면 리더는 안전지대에 머무르지 않고 '학습지대'로 옮겨와야 한다는 내용이었다. 토니는 우선 독서의 중요성에 대해 말했다. 경영과 리더십에 대한 책을 읽음으로써 앞으로 직급이 올랐을 때 그에 대한 역할에 맞는 준비를 할 수 있다는 것이었다.

다음으로 리더는 다른 사람들의 말에 귀를 기울여야 한다고 했다. 예를 들어 외부 세미나와 회의에 참석하거나 차 안에서 동기를 유발하는 테이프를 듣는 것이 도움이 된다고 했다. 덧붙여 토니는 나눔에 대해 얘기했다. 특히 목표를 세우는 것에 대해 좀 더 많은 사람들과 공유하라는 것이었다. 또한 일뿐만 아니라 건강과 가족 등 다른 분야에서도 균형을 유지하라고 충고했다.

마지막으로 토니는 긍정적인 마음의 중요성에 대해 강조하며 마지막 수업을 끝냈다. 나는 그 동안 토니와의 수업 시간에 배웠던 내용들을 정리한 노트를 토니에게 보여주며 토니에게 황동 양동이를 선물했다.

에필로그

　토니와 함께 한 8번의 월요일 아침 수업은 내 인생의 전환점
이 되었다. 6개월 전, 나는 승진했고 내 자리는 제니에게 돌아갔
다. 대부분의 사람들은 토니와 같은 멘토를 만나지 못한다. 나는
당신도 토니의 가르침을 받고 그 가르침을 다른 사람들에게 전
해주길 바란다.

reflected in ~에 반영되다   **acclaim** 갈채하다, 환호하다   **reputation** 명성
premier 1등의, 최고의   **worldwide** 전 세계적으로

· · ·

David has been a featured expert on public television. '데이비드는 TV에
특집으로 다뤄진 전문가이다'

About the Author

David Cottrell, President and CEO of CornerStone Leadership Institute, is an internationally-known leadership consultant, educator, and speaker. His business experience includes senior management positions with Xerox and FedEx. He also led the successful turn-around of a chapter eleven company before founding CornerStone.

David's 25-plus years of professional experience are reflected in eleven highly acclaimed books and his reputation as a premier public speaker. David has been a featured expert on public television and has presented his leadership message to over 25,000 managers worldwide.

He is consistently ranked #1 in conference and keynote evaluations and comments as follows are common:

About the Interpreter

정호섭, 뉴욕주립대에서 국제관계를 전공했다. 재학시절에는 조선일보 뉴욕에서 근무하기도 하였다. 뉴욕에서 여러 업체의 계약관련 업무를 담당했고 현대-기아, 신한-조흥, 엠코, LG-AD 등 많은 기업체에서 비즈니스 강의를 했다. 현재는 YBM 시사에서 비즈니스 영어를 담당하고 있다.

한언의 사명선언문

Since 3rd day of January, 1998

Our Mission

- 우리는 새로운 지식을 창출, 전파하여 전 인류가 이를 공유케 함으로써 인류문화의 발전과 행복에 이바지한다.
- 우리는 끊임없이 학습하는 조직으로서 자신과 조직의 발전을 위해 쉼없이 노력하며, 궁극적으로는 세계적 컨텐츠 그룹을 지향한다.
- 우리는 정신적, 물질적으로 최고 수준의 복지를 실현하기 위해 노력하며, 명실공히 초일류 사원들의 집합체로서 부끄럼없이 행동한다.

Our Vision

한언은 컨텐츠 기업의 선도적 성공모델이 된다.

저희 한언인들은 위와 같은 사명을 항상 가슴 속에 간직하고
좋은 책을 만들기 위해 최선을 다하고 있습니다.
독자 여러분의 아낌없는 충고와 격려를 부탁드립니다.

· 한언 가족 ·

HanEon′s Mission statement

Our Mission

- We create and broadcast new knowledge for the advancement and happiness of the whole human race.
- We do our best to improve ourselves and the organization, with the ultimate goal of striving to be the best content group in the world.
- We try to realize the highest quality of welfare system in both mental and physical ways and we behave in a manner that reflects our mission as proud members of HanEon Community.

Our Vision

HanEon will be the leading Success Model of the content group.